A Catholic Reading Guide to Universalism

A Catholic Reading Guide to Universalism

Robert Wild

Foreword by
Robin A. Parry

RESOURCE *Publications* · Eugene, Oregon

A CATHOLIC READING GUIDE TO UNIVERSALISM

Resource Publications
An Imprint of Wipf and Stock Publishers
199 W. 8th Ave., Suite 3
Eugene, OR 97401

www.wipfandstock.com

ISBN 13: 978-1-4982-2317-1

Manufactured in the U.S.A. 08/14/2015

Dedicated to Hans Urs von Balthasar

The nature of evil is unstable and passes away. It did not come into existence in the beginning with the creation, and it will not continue to exist eternally along with the beings that have ontological consistence. For the beings that derive their existence from the One who is the Being continue to be eternally; but if anything is out of the One who is, its essence is not in Being. This thing, therefore, will pass away and disappear in due course, in the universal restoration [apokatastasis] of all into the Good. As a consequence, in that life which lies before us in hope there will remain no trace of evil which now prevails over us.

—ST. GREGORY OF NYSSA, FATHER AND DOCTOR OF THE CHURCH

Table of Contents

Foreword

THINKING ABOUT HELL IS not as simple as you might imagine. The issues that swirl around this controversial topic are wide-ranging and can be rather complicated. Hell is not just about eschatology—the so-called "last things." It is about the doctrine of God (his love, his justice, his goodness, his omnipotence, etc.), it is about creation, it is about theological anthropology (the image of God), it is about the incarnation, it is about the atoning death and resurrection of Christ, it is about the church and election, and, of course, it *is* about the eschaton: judgment day, new creation, resurrection, theosis, heaven, and hell. When you start to ask "simple" questions—such as "What is hell?" or "Who will go to hell?"—you find that you have opened the lid on a whole mass of interconnected issues, many of which are at the core of Christian theology and identity. Yikes!

In addition to that, a lot of books and articles have been written that touch on the question of hell and universal salvation. Double yikes! Consequently, the daunting task facing anyone coming to consider the issues of hell and universalism is where on earth to start. So it is that Father Wild's new book is to be welcomed for providing a valuable service in offering to serve as a guide through the jungle of issues and literature.

What is so helpful about his book is its breadth:

- *Temporal breadth:* it covers thinkers from the first century through to the twenty-first.

- *Ecumenical breadth:* it represents Catholic, Orthodox, and Protestant perspectives.
- *Breadth of discipline:* it considers biblical, historical, theological, and philosophical works.

What is also refreshing is that Father Wild has restored some Catholic balance to a discussion that has for the past few centuries been too dominated by Protestant voices. And why not get some balance back? So many of the great Christian voices in the past that embraced a "wider hope" were fathers of the church catholic, and some of them were very much in the Latin, Western part of that church. The hope that God will save all people is an ancient orthodox and catholic hope, even if it was eclipsed in the wake of Augustine. It was never condemned as heretical, as Father Wild shows, so there is no good reason why this hope cannot find a place within the Catholic fold today. It is not, nor could it be, *the* Catholic view, but as Father Wild helpfully shows, it can be *a* Catholic view. The twentieth century seems to bear this out in that there have been signs of a welcome, albeit gradual and cautious, Catholic recovery of the hope that God will achieve *all* his purposes for creation. We see this, for instance, in the works of great Catholic theologians like Rahner and Balthasar. So I am hopeful that a belief in universal salvation, a belief that has its roots deep in the Catholic tradition, can be excavated and polished up to serve the needs of contemporary Catholicism.

I am grateful for the help this little book offers readers, especially Catholic readers, in their own explorations in Christian eschatology. I trust that God will use it for his glory.

Dr. Robin A. Parry,
author of *The Evangelical Universalist*
March 23, 2015

Preface

FOR SEVERAL YEARS I have been reading in the area of universalism. (For now, we'll just understand this to mean the belief that everyone will be saved. Further distinctions will follow in the text.) Off and on I thought of writing a book, or an article, or something on this topic. However, as I continued to read, it became very clear that a sufficient amount of material was already available on this subject, and there was no need to try and make my own "creative contribution" to the discussion. I believe most of the important study has been done. Very many people, however, are not familiar with much of the literature I've been reading. I thought a brief *Guide* might be helpful and that I might make a small contribution to a better understanding of universalism.

At the time of this decision I was seventy-seven years old. One of Hans Urs von Balthasar's last books was *Dare We Hope That All Men Be Saved?*[1] I will be frequently referring to this book. For now I simply want to mention that it was the book that started me off on my study of universalism, perhaps seven or eight years ago. Since he wrote this book toward the end of his life, I think that he wanted to say, before he died, something that he considered of extreme importance to the church.

Karl Rahner also said that he wished he had had time to write a book on this topic before he died: "I would still really like to have written something about such a teaching on *apokatastasis* that would be orthodox and acceptable. But it is a very difficult matter. You would probably have to study and

1. Balthasar, *Dare We Hope?*

answer once again new questions in the history of dogma and especially also in exegesis; you would also have to consider questions of exegetical and philosophical interpretation. For all that, my time and strength may not be sufficient anymore."[2] Unfortunately he never got around to writing it: he was seveny-five.

I have something of Balthasar's intention in my closing years. I put "Catholic" in the title because I wish especially to attract the attention of Catholics. I am a Catholic priest, and so I have, of course, a special love for, and responsibility to, my Catholic sisters and brothers. I believe, as well, that Catholics are probably more unfamiliar with the literature available on universalism than other Christians. I have included a number of Catholic (and Orthodox) sources not found in most Protestant literature on this topic. But despite the particular address to Catholics, the book, of course, can be helpful to anyone interested in this subject. Actually, the majority of sources quoted in my *Guide* are Protestant.

When I first read the title of Balthasar's book many years ago my first thought was: "How can you hope for that? What about the teaching of the church? What about hell? What about the words of Christ in the Gospels? What about the private revelations that describe people falling into hell?" And so on. Balthasar's book was the beginning of my study about universalism, which has ended—in my hope that everyone *will* be saved.

In one sense this *Guide* has turned out to be a kind of companion volume to *Dare We Hope?* Considering his age and energy, Balthasar's book is rather sketchy and brief for such a complex subject. This *Guide* seeks to present some of the best arguments from a variety of sources to bolster the arguments Balthasar used to demonstrate his thesis.

I felt theologically comfortable in putting this *Guide* together, although, I'm sure, many of the ideas will scandalize some of my fellow Catholics! I will be in good company. You will see in this book the number of great thinkers, past and present, who were and are universalists.

The negative reactions Balthasar received to his book was one of the reasons for my putting this book together: the adverse responses revealed much ignorance about this topic. But it was not simply the negative reactions to his thesis that motivated me—people are allowed to disagree—but it was the tone and, I might say, the prejudiced and intellectually mindless nature of some of the criticisms he received that embarrassed me. He is considered by many to be one of the outstanding Catholic thinkers of the

2. Phan, *Eternity in Time*, 53.

twentieth century and yet he was labeled as one of those average Catholics who veil the hereafter in a "rose-red fog" and "wishful fantasies," participate "irresponsibly and cruelly in operation mollification" through their "salvation optimism," adopt the "dull and colorless garrulousness of present-day church discourse," practice "modernistic theology," and call for "presumptuous trust in God's mercifulness." So be it; if I have been cast aside as a hopeless conservative by the tribe of the left, then I now know what sort of dung-heap I have been dumped upon by the right.[3]

Coupled with these senseless reactions that Balthasar received were the extremely unintelligent remarks I often read of my Catholic friends toward anyone expressing a belief in universalism. To be quite frank: I was often appalled at their prejudices and ignorance! It seemed that such critics had not read any of the really intelligent studies available on universalism. I concluded that Catholicism in general was very far behind in a scholarly approach to universalism. I still think so. For if Catholic theologians could counter Balthasar with such uninformed objections, what must the majority of Catholics think!

It seems the mainstream of Christians is still under the spell of Augustine and his terrible teaching of *massa damnata* (which we shall be considering). It is because Balthasar dared to present this lifegiving teaching about universalism that I dedicate this book to him. I'm sure he is right about *hoping* for the salvation of all. Hoping can't be heretical! After a few more centuries, his view will certainly become more widespread among Catholics and Christians as it was in the early centuries. Such close-mindedness made me realize even more the necessity to make more widely known what I consider some of the best thinking available about universalism. Thank you, Fr. Hans, for all your magnificent writings, and especially for your book *Dare We Hope?*

I also felt comfortable in compiling this *Guide* because I know I am among a growing number of Christians who believe in some kind of unversalism. The names of scholars who hold this position you will discover in this *Guide*. But I'm sure the number of Christians who believe in universalism is very great. (I gave a homily recently to a monastic community on *Dare We Hope?*, and the abbot afterwards said to me, "That's what I believe.")

My primary goal is not to convince people to become universalists (although, I admit, this is what I desire and pray for!). But most of all I simply

3. *Dare We Hope?*, 19–20.

want to help people become more aware of what is available so they can make up their own minds. Once in a while I may insert my own opinions about what I am presenting, but basically I'm simply trying to make more known the available research on this topic. I am inviting the reader to come to her or his own *informed* conclusions.

I will be presenting mostly the *pros* to universalism. You can find the *cons* to universalism yourself. They are available in an extraordinary amount of literature. Presenting the pros may seem like a prejudice. It is! We have been hearing the cons for most of our lives, but very few people have heard the intelligent pros. I will not attempt to put the material in any too rigid a chronological or topical format. Thus, there may be a fair amount of repetition as often authors make the same arguments for universalism. This repetition can have a desirable accumulative effect in your minds about the arguments.

Also, this is not a scholarly work in the sense that the excerpts I have chosen are meant to be the last word on the subject. They will be scholarly and enlightened opinions, but scholars will certainly disagree on a number of the conclusions presented here. My intention is not to try to present *final arguments* but to heighten the awareness of non-scholarly readers to the major issues involved concerning universalism, and some of the common arguments. The book is meant to whet your appetite for further study, and suggest some references where you may continue to look if you wish. I have become convinced that there is too much *unintelligent thinking* about this topic, and I wish to help to dispel it.

There will probably be one major objection: "Father Wild, you are unsettling the faith of ordinary Catholics by publishing a book about universalism, which we all know is heretical and against the teaching of the church." Well, of course, that's the $64 question. As a result of my study I have come to believe that this is not true—the church has never condemned this doctrine at any *legitimate* council. However, you will see that some of the fathers of the church and theologians down through the ages were cautious in presenting this doctrine for fear it would scandalize and be misunderstood by the faithful. Karl Barth famously said: "I do not teach universalism, but I do not not teach it either." And Jacques Ellul said: "I do not teach universalism, I announce it."[4] They were hesitant in teaching it in too explicit a manner.

4. Ellul, *What I Believe*, 207.

I wish to dispel the prejudice that universalism is some secret doctrine that is only discussed fearfully behind closed theological doors. Not true. Millions of people are thinking about this aspect of our faith, and books, conferences, and articles are proliferating. I don't think universalism is any kind of secret and suspect view that needs to be hushed up and hidden from the eyes of the multitude.

Probably very many people no longer believe in eternal punishment anyhow (!), or in a God who could condemn even one person to such a fate. George MacDonald said that he couldn't believe in a God who would condemn even one person to eternal punishment. Someone said to him that such a doctrine as universal salvation is too good to be true. He replied, "It's so good it *must* be true."[5]

As a Catholic priest it has been my vocation to try and draw people closer to God. It has been my experience, however, that too many people still have terrible ideas about God, and often it's because of the doctrine about hell: "How could a God of love . . ." and so on. As you will see, one of the main motives of those proposing the opinion of universalism from the earliest days of Christianity until the present has been to foster a notion of the goodness of God that corresponds to what St. John told us, that "God is love." In these closing years of my life I want to do what I can to help remove this terrible obstacle to relating to God who is Love.

As a youngster I came across the story of Chicken Little and the Knight who encountered this little bird on the road with his wings held up. "What are you doing?" asked the Knight. "There is a rumor in the animal kingdom that the sky is about to fall, and I'm going to hold it up," replied Chicken Little. "Don't be ridiculous," said the Knight, "if the sky is going to fall there's not much you can do about it." "I know," said the little bird, "but one does what one can."

This story has become one of my inspirational words in life. I know that my *Guide* will not reach very many people, but "one does what one can." I want to make my small contribution to changing the general Christian understanding of the possibility of universalism.

The answer to the question of universalism must be rooted in the person of Jesus and the nature of God, and not in any legalistic, philosophical, or logical theories—and, I may add, not even in such pragmatic

5. "George MacDonald and the Larger Hope: Part 1," Father of the Inklings, http://fatheroftheinklings.com/behind-the-wardrobe/topics-on-gods-justice-the-atonement-and-the-potentiality-of-universal-reconciliation/george-macdonald-and-universal-reconciliation-part-1/ (accessed June 13, 2015).

speculations such as, "It will destroy the missionary mandate of Christ; it will lead to more indifference about being good," and so forth. (These objections will be dealt with in the text.) But these are not theological arguments. They are practical considerations about what such a doctrine *might* cause. The doctrine itself must be built on the nature of Christ's redemptive work and the nature of God. Authors may use the word "universalism" in different ways, but the Christian always understands that the salvation of every person can only come through Jesus Christ.

My approach will be to state some findings about universalism and then give some references. I assure you that what I share here is the result of a fair amount of research and study. If you are able, you can find the documentation for everything in this *Guide* for yourself.

On my shelf I have about twenty or more books on the topic of universalism; and I have a number of articles in my files. They have convinced me to hope and pray for the salvation of all. My hope is that the brief summaries will be sufficient to give you a broad understanding of universalism and the present debate about it.

You may be attracted to read one or several of the books. I believe these books cover all the major aspects of universalism. This survey is not exhaustive and there are, I'm sure, other important books on the subject that I am not aware of. These are books I have read. I believe they are sufficient to stimulate your interest and supply you with enough information for you to make up your own mind and to come to an enlightened position.

I realize that many of the readers of the present book may never have the opportunity to read most of the books quoted, perhaps never even to have them in her or his hands. No matter. I want to convey that there is an enormous amount of writing available on the subject of universalism and that the opinions about it are well thought out and responsible. Universalism was a much-discussed topic in the early centuries of Christian theology and held by many of the faithful. In our times we are witnessing once again the presentation of universalism as a legitimate belief for Christians. It is this awareness I especially wish to foster with this *Guide*.

Countless efforts are made on all fronts to make the knowledge of Christ more effective and available in the world. One of the obstacles to an acceptance of Christ is the belief in hell and the consequent terrible notion of God it fosters. Down through the ages, how many millions of people have been turned away from God by the doctrine of hell? And how many more have been discouraged and rendered hopeless by the teaching that by their actions they are able to determine their everlasting destiny? Do we have the power to even make such a choice?

This book is a very small contribution to removing these obstacles to an acceptance of a loving God. I have been a Catholic all my life. I know how shocking the above paragraph will be to many of my sisters and brothers. But after a fairly long life as a Catholic, and after many years of study and reflection, this is the conclusion I have come to and the teaching I would like to leave to my sisters and brothers in the faith. What a burst of new life would penetrate the human race if everyone believed that God is love and that they were already eternally safe in the arms of Love!

As you have seen, I've dedicated the book to Balthasar. The silence surrounding the dedication says everything.

Finally, the views expressed in this book are those of the author and should in no way be attributed to the Madonna House community to which I belong.

Robert Wild

Easter Sunday, April 5, 2015

Acknowledgments

Permissions granted from Ignatius Press for quotations from Hans Urs von Balthasar, *Dare We Hope That All Men Be Saved? With a Short Discourse on Hell* (San Francisco: Ignatius, 1988).

Permissions granted from *First Things* for quotations from Richard John Neuhaus, "*Will All Be Saved?*" The Public Square.

Permissions granted from Susquehanna University Press for quotations from John Cronen and Eric Reitan, *God's Final Victory* (London: Continuum, 2011).

Permissions granted from Estabon Deak for quotations from *Apokatastasis*. (Toronto: University of St. Michael's College, 1977).

Permissions granted from Princeton University Press for quotations from Pavel Florensky, *The Pillar and Ground of Truth* (Princeton, NJ: Princeton University Press, 1997).

Permissions granted from Brill for quotations from Ilaria Ramelli, *The Christian Doctrine of Apokatastasis* (Leiden: Brill, 2013).

Permissions granted from Oxford University Press for quotations from Gerald O'Collins, *God's other People* (Oxford: Oxford University Press, 2008).

Permissions granted from Wipf and Stock Publishers for quotations from Nicholas Ansell *The Annihilation of Hell* (Eugene, OR: Wipf and Stock, 2013).

Excerpts from *Apokatastasis* by Ilaria Ramelli are reprinted by permission of Koninklijke BRILL NV.

Permissions granted from Wipf and Stock Publishers for quotations from Gregory MacDonald, *The Evangelical Universalist* (Eugene, OR: Wipf and Stock, 2006).

Permissions granted from Wipf and Stock Publishers for quotations from John. A. T. Robinson, *In the End, God* (Eugene, OR: Wipf and Stock, 2011).

Permissions granted from Wipf and Stock Publishers for quotations from Bradley Jersak *Her Gates Will Never Be Shut* (Eugene, OR: Wipf and Stock, 2009).

Permissions granted from St. Vladimir's Seminary Press for quotations from Archbishop Hilarion Alfeyev, *Christ the Conqueror of Hell* (Crestwood, NY: St. Vladimir's Seminary Press, 2009).

Permissions granted from St. Vladimir's Seminary Press for quotations from Archbishop Hilarion Alfeyev *Christ the Conqueror of Hell* (Crestwood, NY: St. Vladimir's Seminary Press, 2009).

Permissions granted from Wipf and Stock Publishers for quotations from Gregory MacDonald, *"All Shall Be Well."* (Eugene, OR: Wipf and Stock, 2011).

Permissions granted from Oxford University Press for quotations from Tom Greggs, *Barth, Origen, and Universal Salvation* (Oxford: Oxford University Press, 2009).

Permissions granted from Oxford University Press for quotations from Morwenna Ludlow, *Universal Salvation, Eschatology in the Thought of Gregory of Nyssa and Karl Rahner* (Oxford: Oxford University Press, 2000).

Permissions granted from Rutherford House for quotations from *Universalism and the Doctrine of Hell*, edited by Nigel M. de S. Cameron (Carlisle, UK: Paternoster, 1992).

— 1 —

Some Interpretive Aids

Definitions of Universalism

What Is Universalism?

PERHAPS THE BEST WAY to begin is to offer a number of definitions of universalism. (Until we come to a more precise definition of *apokatastasis*, the traditional Greek word for universalism, we'll understand *apokatastasis* as "universalism" in general.) If you are going to buy any book, I'd recommend Parry and Partridge's *Universal Salvation?*, the first book from which I will be quoting. They give a good idea of the current debate, and have plenty of references if you wish to study further.

These two editors are among the foremost advocates of Christian universalism. We will come across their views frequently throughout this *Guide* in which, as mentioned in the Preface, I am primarily concerned with making known the views of those who believe in universalism. Thus, in the types of universalism outlined below, I'm mostly interested in *Strong Universalism*. The majority of Christians—and probably most theologians—believe that in the end there will be some people in hell if they do not make the proper acts of faith and repentance. Literature containing such views is quite common and well known. My intention is to make more known the literature that deals with *Strong Universalism*. I begin with the editors' Introduction.

Kinds of Universalism

Multiracial—There is a sense in which *all* Christians could be considered to be "universalists." Since the early days of its existence the Christian church has stood by the claim that God's people are a multicultural group composed of persons of every nation. This view could be labelled "multiracial universalism" and all our contributors would defend it.

Arminian—According to this kind of universalism God desires to save all but he may not actually achieve this. Not all Christians can agree that God desires the salvation of every individual. The Augustinian/Calvinist traditions would maintain that God always achieves his purposes. If God did intend to save every individual then he would do so. Given that only a few respond to the Christian gospel, this must mean that God did not intend to save every individual.

Strong Universalism—God does indeed desire to save everyone, and will achieve his purpose. Thus all individuals will in fact be saved. Strong universalisms can be thought of, for our purposes, as articulated, in at least three forms.

Kinds of Strong Universalism:

Non-Christian—All will eventually come to the "ultimate good." How this good is conceived will vary considerably from one system to the next.

Pluralist—This is the view that sees all major religious systems will eventually lead to the same goal. This view is obviously not compatible with Christian theology in that it achieves its end only by pushing Christ and his atonement to the periphery as merely one route to salvation.

Christian Universalism—Although this is a wide family of views, they share in common (a) the commitment to working within a Christian theological framework and (b) the claim that all individuals will be saved through the work of Christ. It is this kind of universalism that is debated in the following pages.[1]

Another fine distinction to be kept in mind during our survey is that between *apokatastasis* and universalism. It is from another source:

1. Parry and Partridge, *Universal Salvation?*, xv–xvii.

> We introduce a distinction between the doctrine of *apokatastasis* and the existential conviction about universal salvation. We are conscious of the fact that it is not so easy to recognize at first sight and in every instance the difference between these two opinions. Perhaps the most tangible difference lies in the aspect of necessity. The *doctrine of apokatastasis* assumes that someday the entire creation will be brought home to God in full eschatological harmony and peace; whereas universalism, though *believing* the same, refrains from advocating it as a *necessity.* Instead it leaves the door of individual freedom open, theoretically at least.[2]

It will be helpful to begin with the most accepted form of universalism—multiracial—that God's people are a multiracial group composed of persons of every nation and part of the salvific plan. O'Collins says:

> I will take up and explore testimony that illuminates the *universal* scope of God's love and offer of salvation. I want to show that this is a strong and lasting theme. My aim is to set out in detail all the major biblical testimony to the universal scope of God's offer of salvation. The witness of the whole bible to God's universal love is very impressive and should be appropriated much more in contemporary discussion of the other religions and God's other people. The one unavoidable but relatively uncontroversial "ism" that will turn up in the early chapters is universalism, used in the sense of God's benevolence towards everyone.[3]

His comments about the OT witness will be very important for our whole discussion of universalism:

> The OT enjoys a certain advantage over the NT for thinking about the relations of "others" to God. The experience of "others" reflected in the 27 books of the NT cannot match the great variety of experiences, hopes, and wishes derived from Israel's long history and incorporated in the 45 books of the OT. Traditional Judaism, which draws not only on the scriptures but also on rabbinic literature, also offers a generous view not only of the salvation of non-Jews, but also of their co-operation in God's plan.[4]

We commonly assert that the New Testament insights are a more perfected and advanced stage of revelation over the Old Testament.

2. Deak, *Apokatastasis,* 256–57.
3. O'Collins, *Salvation for All,* v–vii.
4. Ibid., vii.

However, what O'Collins is saying is that the Old Testament has a much more generous vision about those "outside" the chosen people; and that these insights should be applied to the New Testament question of those "outside" Christianity.

He then goes through numerous texts in both the Old and New Testaments that witness to God's benevolence to everyone. His chapter titles speak for themselves: "The Universal Benevolence of God"; "Holy Outsiders"; "The Universal Presence of Christ and the Spirit"; "Universal Wisdom"; "Saving Faith and Outsiders."

A few quotes from his concluding chapter will suffice for my purposes. I doubt if anyone reading this present book has problems with God's *benevolence and love toward everyone.* The really controversial question is what is the final stage of this benevolence? Will everyone accept God's offer of salvation or not? But, first, let us present some of the author's conclusions.

Conclusions from Hebrews and Paul

> The faithful obedience of Jesus became God's way of saving human beings. But where does that leave all those innumerable outsiders who do not know Jesus and hence cannot consciously obey him and experience in him the cause/source of their eternal salvation? We presume that the "great cloud of witnesses" (12:1) either by name or in general, were eventually blessed with eternal salvation. Without knowing Jesus and hence without the possibility of consciously obeying him, they mysteriously experienced him (and his Holy Spirit) the cause of their salvation.
>
> Paul deserves the last word. The apostle argues that 'all have sinned and fallen short of the glory/beauty of God (Rom 3:23) before maintaining that all human beings are to be saved by faith (Rom 3:27–31). He returns to these two themes later by saying that "God has imprisoned all in disobedience so that he may be merciful to all" (Rom 11:32).
>
> Faith and merciful salvation are available for all. Paul divides his world into Jews and Gentiles, two groups who have been unfaithful to God. But God makes use of such infidelity to manifest to all his bountiful mercy. Paul envisions the divine mercy going out to all through Jesus Christ and his Spirit. This vision of salvation for all human beings arguably forms the crowning point of Paul's greatest letter. It can rightly serve as the closing words of this

> book: "God has imprisoned all in disobedience so that he may be merciful to all."[5]

As you will see, this is a favorite text for universalists of all stripes. But O'Collins limits himself to emphasizing the universal scope of God's benevolence and does not go into the questions of how or whether all will actually be saved.

Lombardi: God's Universal Salvific Will

The following book is not exactly about universalism but along the lines of O'Collins's book: it concerns God's consequent, primary will (as the theologians define it) to save everyone. Her book gives a brief treatment of how the recent teaching of the Catholic Church and some theologians understand the salvific presence of the Trinity in every person in the world. Thus it is a kind of foundation for *apokatastasis*: if God will eventually save everyone, a theology of how the Trinity is present in everyone is necessary. A brief quote from her conclusion will suffice for my purposes:

> The universal salvific will of God is part of the full doctrine of God and it needs to be taught with clarity and hope. Any suggestion of limitation narrows God's mercy and implies that God's desire to save all people is not universal. If God's intention to save is universal, we must trust that God is acting in all communities and in all people. The wideness of God's mercy must be recovered and proclaimed.
>
> "The theological question today is not whether people who do not belong to the visible Catholic Church can attain salvation. It is theologically certain that they can on certain given conditions. The question is how do they attain salvation." (Cardinal Arinze)
>
> While Christians affirm the uniqueness of Jesus Christ and the universal presence of the Holy Spirit, the acknowledgment of God's saving action outside the boundaries of Christianity has opened the doors to new debates and questions. It appears that the debate hinges on the use of two propositions: *by* and *in*. The church is faced with the implications of three claims studied and addressed by theologians: "People are saved by Jesus Christ *in* the church" (exclusiveness); People are saved by Jesus Christ in their own religious traditions (inclusivism); "People are saved by their own tradition/ mediator in their own traditions" (pluralism). This

5. Ibid., 258–59, 571.

topic remains both challenging and inspiring. The "dialogue of salvation" continues.[6]

What is a theologumenon?

Another focus to keep in mind throughout your reading of this *Guide* is the theological term *theologumenon.* Frequently in the literature here being presented, opinions about universalism can be put in the theological category of *theologumena* and not of *doctrines* or *dogmas* of the church.

Karl Rahner:

> A theologumenon is a proposition expressing a theological statement which cannot be directly regarded as official teaching of the church, as dogma binding in faith, but which is the outcome and expression of an endeavor to understand the faith by establishing connections between binding doctrines of faith and by confronting dogmatic teachings with the whole of secular experience and all a man—or an age—knows.
>
> Such theologumena are absolutely necessary for theology and the formulation of the faith. That can be seen from the mere fact that even the official teaching of the church does not and cannot consist only of dogmas in the strict sense, but enunciates theological statements without (yet) absolutely committing the faith to them. These are theologumena which have become generally accepted, sociologically speaking, in the church. Such theologumena must be made because otherwise actual understanding and really practical efficacy of the articles of faith in the proper sense would not be possible at all. Theologumena are necessary because revelation does not comprise all knowledge of reality in its origin and degrees.
>
> Theology is a history of perpetual changes in theologumena, faster or slower, of greater or less fundamental a kind as the case may be. Ultimately that history is identical with that of man's historical growth in the knowledge of truth.[7]

Obviously, this is only meant to introduce you to the concept of a theologumenon. Parry specifically refers to universalism as a theologumenon.

6. Lombardi, *What Are They Saying About The Universal Salvific Will of God?*, 103–4.
7. Rahner, *Encyclopedia of Theology*, 1685–86.

It will be one of the focuses for our consideration of universalism. Actually, the views about universalism are theologumena and not church doctrine.

Robin Parry:

Universalism occupies a middle ground between dogma and heresy. It is neither a teaching that all orthodox believers are expected to adhere to (in the way that the Trinity, or the union of deity and humanity in the one person of Christ are), nor one that they must avoid.

Perhaps the most appropriate category to employ is that of theologumena. Theologumena are pious opinions that are consistent with Christian dogma. They are neither required nor forbidden.

To see universalism in the category of theologumena means that one cannot preach universalism as "the Christian view" or "the faith of the church" but it also means that one may believe in it and develop a Universalist version of Christian theology.

It is common for theologians to suggest that if *apokatastasis* is a matter of theologumena then, although one is permitted to hope that God will save everybody, one must not go beyond this tentative faith to believe that *God certainly will save all.* Why? Because it is suggested to do so is presumptuous. I must politely disagree.

There are plenty of matters which are theologumena about which a believer may hold strong convictions. For instance, if universalism is theologumena then so is its denial. Yet, I have rarely heard it suggested that a firm conviction that some people will be lost forever is presumptuous or in some way out of order. Indeed, most Christians throughout history have had precisely such a conviction and have felt at perfect liberty to preach it.

When I say that universalism, like its denial, is theologumena, I mean simply that it is an issue about which Christians can legitimately disagree within the boundaries of orthodox Christianity. So whilst I have no problem with some Universalists affirming no more than a hopeful universalism, I can see no good reason to suppose that Christian orthodoxy *requires* such hesitancy.

Speaking for myself, I have no qualms about saying that I am a convinced Universalist. I do believe that the proposition "God will save everyone through Christ" is a true proposition and consequently I think that those who disagree with it are mistaken. However, what I don't believe is that those who disagree with it

> (i.e., almost everybody) are unorthodox, unchristian, unkind, unspiritual, or unclever.
>
> Similarly, whilst I have never preached or taught universalism in a church context, if I were to do so I would not claim, "This is the Christian teaching," or "This is fundamental doctrine" or "This is the faith of the church." I would say, "This is an issue on which devout Christians disagree but here is what I believe and this is why I believe it. You must judge for yourselves, before God, what you think."
>
> So none of this is to suggest that the issue is a matter of indifference, nor that Christians should not debate about the issue—even vigorously. It is simply to relocate the discussion from being a debate between "the orthodox" and "the heretics" and to see it as an in-house theological disagreement. Indeed to see it as an issue that Christians, whilst they might disagree over it, should not divide over it. [8]

The theology of the great father of the church Origen will figure prominently in our discussions. Here I simply note that theologumena were very much a part of his thinking. In the very beginning of his master work, *On First Principles*, Origen makes the distinction between church doctrine and opinions (read theologumena). Often those who criticize his views fail to notice this distinction he made. Many of his statements that were later labeled as "heresies" Origen explicitly presented as *opinions:*

> But the following fact should be understood. The holy apostles, when preaching the faith of Christ, took certain doctrines, namely those which they believed to be necessary ones, and delivered them in the plainest terms to all believers, even to such as appeared to be somewhat dull in the investigation of divine knowledge. The grounds of their statements they left to be investigated by such as should merit the higher gifts of the Spirit and in particular by such as should afterwards receive, through the Spirit himself, graces of language, wisdom and knowledge.
>
> There are other doctrines, however, about which the apostles simply said that things were so, keeping silence as to the how or why; their intentions undoubtedly being as should prove to be lovers of wisdom, with an exercise on which to display the fruit of their ability. The men I refer to are those who train themselves to become worthy and capable of receiving wisdom.[9]

8. Parry, "Universalism as a Theologumenon," 522.

9. Origen, On First Principles, 2.

Balthasar quotes Thielicke on Theologumena

> There are theological truths and circumstances—in this case, the situations of the "lost"—that cannot be subject of dogmatic statements but only contents of prayer. Nothing prevents one from beseeching in prayer that those who have rejected Christ might themselves not be rejected, that their histories might continue together with God in eternity, and that the boundlessness of eternal love should not draw back even before *them.*
>
> Only in that case can the speculative question about the how—whether it is answered through the *Descensus ad inferos* or however—be let out of consideration, while any attempt to formulate a dogmatic proposition here would immediately lead to a profusion of supplementary hypothetical theses.
>
> At the next moment, we would already find ourselves in the midst of fantasy and the manipulation of heavenly-hellish stage sets. But prayer for the "lost" can leave the legitimacy of the requested goal and the means to its attainment up to the hands that this request, like all others, is included under the general proviso: "Thy will be done." This proviso is a declaration of trust.[10]

Eastern Orthodoxy also recognizes the presence of theologumena in tradition.

Alfeyev

"Personal opinions (*theologoumena)* of individual church writers, however respected they may be, are not always representative of church doctrine. This section [in his book] attempts to distinguish which parts of the examined texts belong to the general doctrine of the Orthodox Church and which parts are personal opinions."[11]

Sergius Bulgakov

Bulgakov is considered by many to be the greatest Orthodox theologian of the twentieth century. His introduction to his eschatology is worth considering as it is a profound correction to an over-rationalistic, an over-dogmatizing approach to the ultimate mysteries of our faith. When he speaks of

10. Balthasar, *Dare We Hope?*, 36–37.

11. Alfeyev. *Christ the Conqueror of Hell*, 205.

"church" he is referring, of course, to the Orthodox Church; but his comments are instructive for the whole ongoing Christian theological tradition.

> The church has not established a single universally obligatory dogmatic definition in the domain of eschatology, if we do not count the brief testimony of the Nicaeno-Constantinople Creed. All the rest, referring to various aspects of eschatology, has not been defined dogmatically; it is an object of dogmatic doctrine that has yet to undergo free theological investigation.
>
> If it is maintained that the absence of an ecclesial definition is compensated by the existence of a firm ecclesial tradition, patristics and otherwise, one must call such an assertion inaccurate or even completely erroneous. Aside from the fact that this tradition is insufficient and disparate, the most important thing here is the *absence of a single tradition.*
>
> By its essence, eschatology deals with a domain of being that transcends the present world and is not measurable solely by the measure of this world. Rationalism seeks to eliminate, simplify, coarsen the contradictions of eschatology; in a word, it seeks to rationalize them.
>
> Rationalism totally rejects antinomic thought [for the concept of "antimony" cf. Pavel Florensky, below] which is characteristic of eschatology. This also removes other possibilities of being than those which are accessible to its present state; that is, being mystery, which transcends its present state, is rejected. But it is precisely the premise of this mystery that lies at the basis of eschatology. Such a two-dimensional thinking also manifests itself in eschatological exegetics, in which it suppresses the antinomism of eschatological texts. It adapts these texts to the life of this aeon, translates them into the language of our world, and lays them on the Procrustean bed of a thought that is inappropriate to its object. Owing to such a translation, eschatology is made to approach the empirical being of our world, but it loses its force and acuteness.
>
> Rationalism is nothing but anthropomorphism in thought. In contrast to the true anthropological principle, anthropomorphism in theology consists in the application of the limited human measure to the divine domain. This is particularly the case in the doctrine of judgment and punishment. Thanks to this anthropomorphism, eschatology stops being what it is and what it should be, the ontology and anthropology revealed in the final destinies of man. The ontological statement of the problem is replaced by a juridical one, and the mysteries of God's love are measured according to the penal code.

> There are mysteries of the future age, unfathomable destinies and untraceable paths of God (Rom 11:33), that are perhaps not destined to be fully revealed in this age. Of course, by way of practical guidance, there remains God's injunction and promise: "ask, and it shall be given you; seek ye shall find; knock, and it shall be opened unto you" (Matt 7:7) but one must also make a place for God's mystery.[12]

Rahner's Hermeneutics of Eschatological Assertions

Before we get into the specific scriptural and theological arguments for *apokatastasis* it will be helpful at this point to introduce one of the most frequently quoted articles by those reflecting on the eschata. It is Karl Rahner's "The Hermeneutics of Eschatological Assertions." [13]

The theses he presents are important theological glasses that can enable you to get a better perspective on the various (especially biblical) theories about universalism. Many scholars have found these views of Rahner's helpful in coming to their conclusions; I thought you might also. They have helped me. However, these glasses may give you a *different* vision from many of the authors quoted here. In any case, they will help you come to a more educated point of view.

Karl Rahner is not easy to read or understand! I originally began this *Guide* with his views, but I thought they might discourage you from continuing to read the rest of my book! So I put them here, just before you are presented with the main arguments.

Peter Phan, Commentary

For a presentation of these assertions, and with a commentary, I turn to Peter Phan, an acknowledged Rahnerian scholar. The quotes within the text are from Rahner.

> Rahner's hermeneutical recommendations, first, demonstrate the almost unmanageable complexity of the task of determining and systematizing the contents of biblical eschatology. Secondly, they underline Rahner's conviction that one should abandon the naïve proof-text approach to biblical eschatology. Thirdly,

12. Bulgakov, *The Bride of the Lamb.* 379–82, 455.
13. In *Theological Investigations*, 4:323–46.

the hermeneutical principles for eschatological assertions must not be imported from outside or conceived a priori but must be formulated on the basis of biblical eschatology itself. And finally, hermeneutics is regarded not as a merely philosophical analysis of biblical texts, but as a properly theological task to be carried out on the basis of the *analogia fidei*. Rahner's first four theses deal with the genuinely future character of Christian eschatological realities. These are known by God and can be revealed to humanity, but essentially hidden and uncontrollable since their outcome depends on the freedom of God and of human beings.

First thesis: "The Christian understanding of the faith and its expression must contain an eschatology which really bears on the *future,* that which is still to come, in a very ordinary, empirical sense of the word time." For Rahner, eschatology deals with realities still to come, realities that belong not only to the ultramundane future but also to the Absolute Future. In interpreting eschatological assertions we must keep this future in mind and cannot dismiss them as mere symbolizations of presently occurring realities.

Second Thesis: "The Christian understanding of the nature, life and personal being of God takes his omniscience not merely as a metaphysical axiom, but as a strict truth of faith, and makes it include God's knowledge of future events. Insofar as this knowledge embraces the realities of the world and mankind, there can be no denying or doubting, in metaphysics or theology, the fundamental abstract possibility of the communication of such future events; they are known by God and they are human, and hence do not of themselves in principle go beyond the capacity of human understanding."

Two points are made in this second thesis: eschatological assertions are not the result of philosophical speculation but are made known by God in a concrete history of revelation and salvation; nevertheless, it is possible and necessary to define the framework within which God's communication about future events can be understood.

Third Thesis (First part): "It is certain from Scripture that God has *not* revealed to humanity the day of the end." Eschatological events have an essentially hidden character so that they are revealed *as* hidden, as unexpected, as mystery. Any hermeneutics of eschatological assertions that regards them as predictions or anticipated report of future events must therefore be false.

Third Thesis (Second part): "If human beings are beings involved in history, they cannot understand themselves in any given present moment without an aetiological retrospect toward a genuinely temporal past, an anamnesis, and without prospect of a genuinely temporal future. Their self-understanding embraces the beginning and the end of their temporal history, both in the life of the individual person and of humanity." The knowledge of the future is an inner dimension of the self-understanding of persons in their present moment of existence and grows out of it.

Fourth Thesis: "Knowledge of the future will be knowledge of the futurity of the present: eschatological knowledge is knowledge of the eschatological present. An eschatological assertion is not an additional, supplementary statement appended to an assertion about the present and the past of the human person but an inner moment of this person's self-understanding." Because man ex-sists into the future, the future in its hiddenness must be a real moment of the present self-understanding of the person. Indeed it can be known and understood *only out of the present*; it is the futurity of the present; it is anthropology conjugated in the future tense.

Fifth Thesis: "We may say that biblical eschatology must always be read as an assertion based on the revealed present and pointing toward the genuine future, but not as an assertion pointing back from an anticipated future into the present. To read from the present out into the future is eschatology, to read from the future back into the present is apocalyptic, which is either phantasy or Gnosticism."

This thesis no doubt constitutes the heart of Rahner's hermeneutics of eschatology. First of all, the source of Christian eschatology for Rahner is the present situation of salvation, which consists in God's Trinitarian self-disclosure to humans in the grace of the crucified and risen Christ. "The Sitz im Leben," says Rahner, "the setting of eschatological assertions is therefore the experience of God's salvific action on *us* in Christ." Whatever the Christians know about their future fulfillment, they know it from the fulfillment that has already occurred in Christ.

Sixth Thesis: "The eschatology of salvation and of loss is not on the same plane. True eschatological discourse must exclude the presumptuous knowledge of a universal *apokatastasis* and of the certainty of the salvation of the individual *before* his death as well as certain knowledge of a damnation which has actually ensued." If eschatology is a transposition of the present existential situation of human beings into its mode of fulfillment, and if this situation is one of salvation and sin, then one should speak of the open, real possibilities of salvation *and* loss for each human being. Hence the exclusion of universal *apokatastasis* as a statement of fact and of the certainty of the salvation of the individual before his death.

Summary: "Christ himself is the hermeneutical principle of all eschatological assertions. Anything that cannot be read and understood as a christological assertion is not a genuine eschatological assertion." Christology is therefore the criterion of the hermeneutics of eschatology. Rahner's eschatology, like Barth's, is decidedly Christocentric. Further, one can see here the unity and compactness of Rahner's anthropology, theology, Christology, and eschatology, with Christology holding the center. To speak about humanity is to speak about God and vice versa. But one cannot speak about humanity and God except in the true God-man, Jesus. And when this Christ-talk is conjugated in the future tense, eschatology emerges.[14]

14. Phan, *Eternity in Time*, 67–76.

— 2 —

The History of Universalism

J. W. Hanson

HANSON WAS ONE OF the studies that launched me on my own in-depth study of universalism. I was amazed at the date—1899—that so much study in the modern period—only a hundred years ago—had been done on this topic. Some of his conclusions presented here have been corrected by more recent studies, but it is my opinion that this is still one of the best historical presentations of universalism in the early centuries. It is a gold mine of reflection and pointers to further study.

Often, when other scholars mention this work—which shows they considered it an important study—their major criticism is that the author has over-simplified his thesis: that universalism in the early centuries was the *predominant belief*. They may be right. And yet, Hanson documents everything he asserts, and his documentation is impressive and quite overwhelming. Again, more recent research may correct this or that historical note, but I highly recommend it as a very good beginning to the study of the historical roots of universalism. From Hanson:

> The purpose of this book is to present some of the evidence of the prevalence in the early centuries of the Christian church, of the doctrine of the final holiness of all mankind. The author has aimed to present irrefragable proofs that the doctrine of Universal Salvation was the prevalent sentiment of the primitive Christian church. The opinions of Christians in the first few centuries should predispose us to believe in their truthfulness, inasmuch as they

> were nearest to the divine Fountain of our religion. The doctrine of Universal Salvation was nowhere taught until *they* inculcated it. Where could they have obtained it but from the source whence they claim to have derived it—the New Testament? The author believes that the following pages show that Universal Restitution was the faith of the early Christians for at least the First Five Hundred Years of the Christian era. [1]

Let me emphasize again before giving Hanson's conclusions that this *Guide* is not meant to be the most scholarly up to date presentation of opinions. Scholars will have objections to some of Hanson's conclusions. My purpose is simply to familiarize you with some of the main areas relevant to the discussion about universalism we shall encounter in this *Guide*, and indicate directions for your own future study and exploration. The summary of Hanson's conclusions:

> A few of the many points established in the foregoing pages may here be named:
>
> 1. During the First Century the primitive Christians did not dwell on matters of eschatology, but devoted their attention to apologetics; they were chiefly anxious to establish the fact of Christ's advent, and of its blessings to the world. Possibly the question of destiny was an open one, till Paganism and Judaism introduced erroneous ideas, when the New Testament doctrine of the *apokatastasis* was asserted, and universal restoration became an accepted belief, as stated later by Clement and Origen, A.D. 180–230.
> 2. The Catacombs give us the views of the unlearned, as Clement and Origen state the doctrine of scholars and teachers. Not a syllable is found hinting at the horrors of Augustinianism, but the inscription on every monument harmonizes with the Universalism of the early fathers.
> 3. Clement declares that all punishment, however severe, is purificatory; that even the 'torments of the damned' are curative. Origen explains even *Gehenna* as signifying limited and curative punishment, and both, as all the other ancient Universalists, declare that "everlasting" (*aionion*) punishment is consonant with universal salvation. So that it is no proof that other primitive Christians who are less explicit as to the final result, taught endless punishment when they employ the same terms.

1. Hanson, www.tentmaker.org. prevailing.

4. Like our Lord and his Apostles, the primitive Christians avoided the words with which the Pagans and Jews defined endless punishment *aidios* or *adialeipton timoria* (endless torment), a doctrine the latter believed, and knew how to describe; but they, the early Christians, called punishment, as did our Lord, *kolasis aionios*, discipline, chastisement, of indefinite, limited duration.
5. The early Christians taught that Christ preached the Gospel to the dead, and for that purpose descended into Hades. Many held that he released all who were there. This shows that repentance beyond the grave, perpetual probation, was then accepted, which precludes the modern error that the soul's destiny is decided at death.
6. Prayers for the dead were universal in the early church, which would be absurd, if their condition is unalterably fixed at the grave.
7. The idea that false threats were necessary to keep the common people in check, and that the truth might be held esoterically, prevailed among the earlier Christians, so that there can be no doubt that many who seem to teach endless punishment, really held the broader views, as we know the most did, and preached terrors pedagogically.
8. The first comparatively complete systematic statement of Christian doctrine ever given to the world was by Clement of Alexandria, A.D. 180, and universal salvation was one of the tenets.
9. The first complete presentation of Christianity as a system was by Origen (A.D. 220) and universal salvation was explicitly contained in it.
10. Universal salvation was the prevailing doctrine in Christendom as long as Greek, the language of the New Testament, was the language of Christendom.
11. Universalism was generally believed in the best centuries, the first three, when Christians were most remarkable for simplicity, goodness and missionary zeal.
12. Universalism was least known when Greek, the language of the New Testament was least known, and when Latin was the language of the church in its darkest, most ignorant, and corrupt ages.
13. Not a writer among those who describe the heresies of the first three hundred years intimates that Universalism was then a

heresy, though it was believed by many, if not by a majority, and certainly by the greatest of the fathers.

14. Not a single creed for five hundred years expresses any idea contrary to universal restoration, or in favor of endless punishment.
15. With the exception of the arguments of Augustine (A.D. 420), there is not an argument known to have been framed against Universalism for at least four hundred years after Christ, by any of the ancient fathers.
16. While the councils that assembled in various parts of Christendom anathematized every kind of doctrine supposed to be heretical, no oecumenical council, for more than five hundred years, condemned Universalism, though it had been advocated in every century by the principal scholars and most revered saints.
17. As late as A.D. 400, Jerome says "most people" (*plerique*), and Augustine "very many" (*quam plurimi*), believed in Universalism, notwithstanding that the tremendous influence of Augustine, and the mighty power of the semi-pagan secular arm, were arrayed against it.
18. The principal ancient Universalists were Christian born and reared, and were among the most scholarly and saintly of all the ancient saints.
19. The most celebrated of the earlier advocates of endless punishment were heathen born, and led corrupt lives in their youth. Tertullian one of the first, and Augustine, the greatest of them, confess to having been among the vilest.
20. The first advocates of endless punishment, Minucius Felix, Tertullian and Augustine, were Latins, ignorant of Greek, and less competent to interpret the meaning of Greek Scriptures than were the Greek scholars.
21. The first advocates of Universalism, after the Apostles, were Greeks, in whose mother-tongue the New Testament was written. They found their Universalism in the Greek Bible. Who should be correct, they or the Latins?
22. The Greek Fathers announced the great truth of universal restoration in an age of darkness, sin and corruption. There was nothing to suggest it to them in the world's literature or religion. It was wholly contrary to everything around them. Where else could they have found it, but where they say they did, in the Gospel?

23. All ecclesiastical historians and the best biblical critics and scholars agree to the prevalence of Universalism in the earlier centuries.
24. From the days of Clement of Alexandria to those of Gregory of Nyssa and Theodore of Mopsuestia (A.D. 180–428), the great theologians and teachers, almost without exception, were Universalists. No equal number in the same centuries were comparable to them for learning and goodness.
25. The first theological school in Christendom, that in Alexandria, taught Universalism for more than two hundred years.
26. In all Christendom, from A.D. 170 to 430, there were six Christian schools. Of these four, the only strictly theological schools, taught Universalism, and but one endless punishment.
27. The three earliest Gnostic sects, the Basilidians, the Carpocratians and the Valentinians (A.D. 117–132) are condemned by Christian writers, and their heresies pointed out, but though they taught Universalism, that doctrine is never condemned by those who oppose them. Irenaeus condemned the errors of the Carpocratians, but does not reprehend their Universalism, though he ascribes the doctrine to them.
28. The first defense of Christianity against Infidelity (Origen against Celsus) puts the defense on Universalistic grounds. Celsus charged the Christians' God with cruelty, because he punished with fire. Origen replied that God's fire is curative; that he is a "Consuming Fire," because he consumes sin and not the sinner.
29. Origen, the chief representative of Universalism in the ancient centuries, was bitterly opposed and condemned for various heresies by ignorant and cruel fanatics. He was accused of opposing Episcopacy, believing in pre-existence, etc., but never was condemned for his Universalism. The very council that anathematized "Origenism" eulogized Gregory of Nyssa, who was explicitly a Universalist as was Origen. Lists of his errors are given by Methodius, Pamphilus and Eusebius, Marcellus, Eustathius and Jerome, but Universalism is not named by one of his opponents. Hippolytus (A.D. 320) names thirty-two known heresies, but Universalism is not mentioned as among them. Epiphanius, "the hammer of heretics," describes eighty heresies, but he does not mention universal salvation, though Gregory of Nyssa, an outspoken Universalist, was, at the time he wrote, the most conspicuous figure in Christendom.

30. Justinian, a half-pagan emperor, who attempted to have Universalism officially condemned, lived in the most corrupt epoch of the Christian centuries. He closed the theological schools, and demanded the condemnation of Universalism by law; but the doctrine was so prevalent in the church that the council refused to obey his edict to suppress it. Lecky says the age of Justinian was "the worst form civilization has assumed."
31. The first clear and definite statement of human destiny by any Christian writer after the days of the Apostles includes universal restoration, and that doctrine was advocated by most of the greatest and best of the Christian Fathers for the first five hundred years of the Christian Era.
32. In one word, a careful study of the early history of the Christian religion will show that the doctrine of universal restoration was least prevalent in the darkest, and prevailed most in the most enlightened, of the earliest centuries—that it was the prevailing doctrine in the Primitive Christian church. [2]

The next article is frequently quoted in *apokatastasis* studies. It covers mostly Origen and the two Gregories—Nyssa and Nazianzus. Sachs's conclusion is the more common one as regards the predominance of the *apokatastasis* theory in the early centuries:

> In retrospect they [the three fathers mentioned above] might be called the "minority report," but their instincts have proven correct insofar as much of the reinterpretation of the nature and purpose of divine punishment and what might, at the very least, be called a justified "bias" in the direction of universal salvation have become part and parcel of contemporary Catholic eschatology. Theological efforts of today, which attempt to correct the pessimistic exaggerations of the past and the frightful images of God to which they gave rise, are not to be dismissed as a modern "sellout" or watering down of the gospel. I hope I have shown how deeply rooted they are in early Christian theology. The history of theology shows how difficult it is to systematize Christian belief in both the reality of human freedom and the sovereignty of divine grace. Indeed, theological reflection on the nature, possibilities, and limits of human freedom remains an important task for the future. But in the end, these patristic voices, echoed as they are in much current theology, remind us that we can and must hope that all will be saved. And the "reason for our hope" (1 Pet 3:15)

2. Ibid.

> is the incomprehensible mystery of God's love itself, not a perfect theological synthesis.[3]

The following book is frequently quoted by scholars in reference not only to *apokatastasis* in the first Christian centuries but to all the other aspects of the eschata as well. I give here only the author's conclusion about *apokatastasis* in the early church.

> Another disputed point, at the end of the Patristic age and beyond, was the actual *extent of eschatological salvation.* Origen's clear hope for the salvation of all spiritual creatures—*the apokatastasis panton*—[restoration of all] was shared openly by Gregory of Nyssa and Evagrius, as well as by some sixth-century anti-Chalcedonian writers, but bitterly contested by others from Origen's time onwards. Jerome, even after his repudiation of Origen in 394, continued to argue that at least all Christian believers will experience the final mercy of God. Augustine assumed, on the other side, that the majority of human beings will not be saved and that even the perseverance of believers in the life of grace is far from assured. Both positions have found their passionate defenders throughout Christian history, and continue to be proposed in our own time. Both remain enshrouded in the double, mutually limiting mystery of God's providential love and the genuineness of human freedom.[4]

Another of Daley's general conclusions is also relevant to our discussion of *apokatastasis:* it would be one of the "serious areas of unresolved disagreement" he mentions here:

> To return to our starting question: can one legitimately speak of 'the hope of the early church'? If one seeks such a hope in the finished form of conciliar definitions, or of an articulated and widely shared theological system, the answer is clearly no; the eschatological consensus we have sketched out here was far less well formed, far less consciously enunciated, in the Patristic centuries, than was the orthodox Christian doctrine of God or of the person of Christ. Nevertheless, the expectations of early Christians for the future formed, on the whole, a remarkably consistent picture, despite serious areas of unresolved disagreement.
>
> The reason, I suggest, is that beyond the influence of apocalyptic speculation and Platonic philosophy, of classical poetry and of pagan folklore—all of which clearly had their influence on

3. Sachs, *Apokatastasis in Patristic Theology,* 7–8.
4. Daley, *The Hope of the Early Church,* 222.

> the church's articulation of its belief—the real basis of Christian hope for the future is the experience of Christians now: the sense that as disciples of Jesus, who is risen, they are already sharers in a larger, richer stream of life, whose full dimensions lie hidden from their minds. Living within history and affirming its lasting value because it has become, in Christ, God's history, the Christian conceives of this history as capable of finally revealing God's plan for the fullness of time (Eph. 1.10). Christ, who fulfilled that plan in time, is understood to be God's norm and agent of judgment, too. Christ's resurrection becomes for his disciples in every age, the promise of resurrection for all humanity; Christ's summons to join his way becomes an invitation to share in the purification and growth that must precede a share in the Kingdom he reveals.
>
> From the vantage point of faith in the risen Lord, the human time is wrapped in eternal love; the many hopes that rise—gropingly, picturesquely—in the heart of the believer are really only attempts to articulate in words the one abiding "mystery, which is Christ in you, your hope of glory" (Col 1.27). It is as an expression of the mystery of Christ that all Christian eschatology finds its unity and its meaning.[5]

Ramelli, Definition of Apocatastasis, Clement of Alexandria's Use of Scripture

The next book, Ilaria L. E. Ramelli's *The Christian Doctrine of Apokatastasis: A Critical Assessment from the New Testament to Eriugena,* (2013) is 890 pages long (!). For the foreseeable future it will be *the indispensable study of universalism up until the eighth century.* (Where you find a disagreement between Ramelli and Hanson, the former's opinions will be considered as the more authoritative.) Ramelli is one of the foremost patristic scholars in the world today. In this survey she treats every Christian author in this timeframe and his or her position on the doctrine of *apokatastasis.* This book alone would be sufficient for your understanding of these centuries.

In lieu of this book not being available to you, I've decided to give you,

1. an outline of the book
2. her understanding of *apokatastasis*
3. Clement of Alexandria's use of Scripture on this topic

5. Ibid., 223–24.

4. her summary of the supposed condemnation of Origen
5. some of her conclusions.

Outline of the book:

1. The Roots of the Doctrine of *Apokatastasis*
2. Origen's First Followers in Alexandria and the East, and his First "Detractors."
3. Origen's Apologists and Followers, the Cappadocians, Evagrius, the Antiochenes, and Fourth-Century Latin Origenians.
4. From Augustine to Eriugena: Latin, Greek, and Syrian Receptions of Origen's Apokatastasis Theory.

Definition of *Apokatastasis*

> The noun *apokatastasis,* related to the verb *apokathistemi,* "I restore, reintegrate, reconstitute, return," bears the fundamental meaning of "restoration, reintegration, reconstitution." This term had a variety of applications in antiquity, but as a Christian and a late-antique philosophical doctrine . . . it came to indicate the theory of universal restoration, that is, of the return of all beings, or at least all rational beings or all humans, to the Good, i.e., God, in the end.
>
> From Origen's *Commentary of John*: "The end will be at the so-called *apokatastasis* in that no one, then, will be left an enemy, if it is true that 'he must reign until he has put all his enemies under his feet, while the last enemy will be radically eliminated: death."
>
> It is to be noted that Origen himself in this passage defines *apokatastasis* as "the so-called *apokatastasis,*" indicating that he is taking this term from a tradition. Now, I think this tradition is represented not only by Clement of Alexandria . . . but also by the NT, and in particular Acts 3:21, in which the key term *apokatastasis* appears and designates restoration, as I shall argue.[6]

Clement of Alexandria is invariably pointed out as the first Christian father to speak about *apokatastasis* and sometimes it is averred that

6. Ramelli, *The Christian Doctrine of Apokatastasis,* 1–4.

he originally obtained this doctrine from outside the Christian tradition. Ramelli disagrees.

Clement of Alexandria

Clement's Use of Scripture

Clement was the first Christian writer to suggest, with great caution, the . . . prospect of universal salvation for all intelligent creatures. The only texts that unquestioningly provided Clement of Alexandria with an explicit rationale for the universal apokatastasis are 1 John 2:2 and Phil 2:10. He did not cite other texts that are conceivable candidates for use as proof texts for universal salvation.

However, Clement frequently teaches, from the scriptures, that God intends to save everyone and invites all to this salvation. However, nothing in this biblical argument . . . offers direct support for the idea that all rational creatures will ultimately be saved. Although the paucity of appeals to the biblical materials might suggest a source other than Scripture (such as Middle Platonic philosophical presuppositions) as the primary motivation for Clement's thought in this area, the relationship between biblical exegesis and concepts consistent with *apokatastasis* to Scripture should be considered more comprehensively than a narrow focus on unambiguous expressions of the concept might indicate.

The Nature and Duration of Punishment after Death.

Five aspects of Clement's understanding of eschatological punishment need to be probed for a relationship to biblical texts: a) the conclusion that punishment after death is redemptive in nature and limited in duration; b) the portrayal of punishment as pedagogical; c) the portrayal of punishment as medicinal; d) the portrayal of punishment as discerning [that is, destroying only that which is evil and not that which is good]; e) redemptive punishment as consistent with the character of God. God's remedial punishment is also part of his goodness.

Conclusion in Clement

The concept of a universal restoration of all rational creatures accomplished through eschatological punishment that is redemptive in nature and limited in duration is rarely articulated explicitly in Clement, and only once is it directly substantiated with biblical texts (1 John 2:2 and Phil 2:10).

Clement of Alexandria, Origen, and Gregory of Nyssa shared in common the hopeful belief that God would ultimately reconcile all rational creatures to God. At the core of their distinctively crafted arguments for this conviction is a common trio of rationales. First, each maintained that evil is inherently finite and, owing to its parasitic relationship to the good, will ultimately pass into nonexistence. Second, each posited a period of remedial punishment that will remove the parasitic accretions of evil from God's creatures so that only the good remains. Third, each believed that the Scriptures taught these things. As thinkers whose minds were shaped first and foremost through their reading of the bible, this third rationale was the most significant. The more subtle understanding of the Scriptures that led Clement, Origen, and Gregory to discern in the biblical story a universal restoration as the story's most fitting conclusion is both a common features of their understanding of the *apokatastasis* and the aspect of it that most clearly highlights the distinctiveness of each theologian's arguments for the concept.

Whatever the other sources for the development of their concepts of universal salvation may have been, it is certain that Clement, Origen, and Gregory believed their ideas to be firmly rooted in the Scriptures. Evaluation of whether they were right in this reading of the biblical text is more appropriately the task of a study in biblical or systematic theology than of this inquiry in historical theology.[7]

Origen

Invariably, when universalism is brought up, someone will say, "Wasn't somebody named Origen condemned for such a teaching—apoca . . . something? And didn't some Council condemn him?" For too many Christians, this is all they know about universalism! Yes, the teaching of the great church father Origen is fundamental to any discussion of universalism.

7. Ibid., 119–36.

And he is considered to be the main inspiration for this doctrine in Christian tradition. To his teaching we now turn.

Greggs

There are a number of scholarly texts I could have chosen to present a summary of Origen's teaching on *apokatastasis* (such as the magisterial work by Ramelli), but I chose Greggs because he gives a succinct account of Origen's teaching and because later on we will consider Greggs's understanding of Barth's view of *apokatastasis*. (Quotes within the text are from Origen unless otherwise noted.)

> Restoration—*apokatastasis* and universalism
>
> The doctrine for which Origen is most (in)famous is the universal restoration of all things, *apokatastasis*. Here, the important word for our purposes of enquiring into preexistence is "restoration"—a return to how things were originally: "when the Son is said to be subjected to the Father the perfect restoration of the entire creation is announced, so when his enemies are said to be subjected to the Son of God we are to understand this to involve the salvation of those subjected and the restoration of those that have been lost." Eschatology is seen as the "perfect restoration (*restitutio*) of the whole of creation" which includes the 'restoration (*reparatio*) of the lost." Both *restitutio and reparatio* have the sense of returning to something that was before.
>
> This theme of restoration can be noted elsewhere in Origen's writings: "I think the stopping point and goal is in the so-called restoration because no one is left as an enemy then, if indeed the statement is true, 'For he must reign until he has put all his enemies under his feet. But the last enemy to be destroyed is death.'" For Origen, the end seems to involve a universal reinstatement, since there then remains *no* enemy against whom to fight. It appears indeed to be the time when God will be "all in all": "that, when 'God be all in all,' they [all creatures] also, since they are a part of all, may have God even in themselves, as he is in all things." What takes place in salvation is the soul becoming a second time what it was before:
>
> "Now I think that since the end and consummation of the saints will happen in those worlds that are not seen and are eternal, we must suppose, from a contemplation of this end . . . that rational creatures have also had a *similar* beginning. And if they had a beginning that was such as they expect their end to be, they

have undoubtedly existed right from their beginning in those worlds 'that are not seen and are eternal.'"

Although the reference here is to the "consummation of the saints," one is immediately directed to the broader category of "rational creatures"; and in both cases, one is directed to an end which will be like the beginning.

This means that punishment in Origen's theology is not absolute. Its purpose is instead to reform the soul. Although Origen does discuss those "separated from every gleam of intelligence or reason" who will be clothed in darkness and live as if in a prison, there is little sense of a permanent hell in Origen's thought. Origen's sense of the graciousness of God always allows for a further opportunity in future aeons. Even the "worst sinner, who has blasphemed the Holy Spirit and been ruled by sin from beginning to end in the whole of this present age, will afterwards in the age to come be brought into order. I know not how."

Those seemingly beyond any salvation in the present age will receive grace in the future. The will of God must be done for the unjust as well as for the just. Thus, just as Paul considers himself to be "all things to all," so too "the Saviour . . . in a way much more divine than Paul, has become 'all things to all,' that he might either 'gain' or perfect 'all things.'" Origen continues:

"The Saviour, therefore, is first and the last, not that he is not what lies between, but it is stated in the terms of extremities to show that he himself has become 'all things.' But consider whether the 'last' is man, or those called the underworld beings, of which the demons also are a part, either in their entirety or some of them."

Being first and last does not involve only temporality, but points to a personal understanding: the Saviour is first and last to everything in salvation—an angel to angels, a human to humans and so on. Salvation thus seems even to stretch (in speculation at least) to the demonic. The work of the Logos cannot be limited. Origen is insistent that Jesus came for the benefit of (at least) the whole human race.

It seems that all things will receive salvation and that they are brought together in a unity in which all things become one:

Finally, when the world was in need of variety and diversity, matter lent itself to the fashioning of the diverse aspects and classes of things in wholly obedient service to the Maker, as to its Lord and Creator, that from it he might produce the diverse forms of things heavenly and earthly. But when events have begun to hasten towards the idea of all things being one as the Father is one with the son, we are bound to believe as a logical consequence that where all are one there will no longer be any diversity.

Jean Danielou argues that the church does not reject *apokatastasis* outright in the anathematization of the fifth ecumenical council—only the Platonic distortion of it: *apokatastasis* "in Christ" is considered by him to be orthodox. Origen's universalism is focused on the particularity of the Christian faith and allows for all of the particularities of creation.[8]

Danielou's comment leads us to this important question: Was Origen ever condemned by the church?

The so-called "condemnation of Origen" by the church [instigated by the Emperor Justinian] in the sixth century probably never occurred properly, and even if it occurred it did so only as a result of a long series of misunderstandings. The 'condemnation' was triggered by the development of a radical kind of Origenism, which he mistook for Origen's own doctrine. The doctrines condemned—which were not Origen's—were the pre-existence of bare souls and the sphericity of the risen body.

Justinian's Letter to the Synod about Origen in fact includes nothing of Origen's true thought among the doctrines it blames. Justinian's statements are impossible to refer to Origen's thought which they misrepresent so heavily.

The Council that is usually cited as that which 'condemned Origen' is the fifth ecumenical council, the second Constantinople Council, in 553 CE. [St. John Paul II will refer to this council below]. First of all, its ecumenicity is in fact doubtful, since it was wanted by Justinian and not by Vigilius, the Bishop of Rome, or other bishops; Vigilius was even brought to Constantinople by force, by the emperor's order, and moreover he did not accept to declare that the council was open. (Justinian had to do so). The anathemas, fifteen in number, were already prepared before the opening of the council.

One of these previously formulated anathemas, which only waited to be ratified by the Council, was against the *apokatastasis* doctrine: "If anyone supports the monstrous doctrine of *apokatastasis*, be it anathema." Origen is not the object of any authentic anathema. Origen was never formally condemned by any Christian ecumenical Council. We may add that Origen, strictly speaking, did not even suffer any formal expulsion from the church. [9]

8. Greggs, *Barth, Origen, and Universal Salvation*, 68–72, 84.

9. Ramelli, *The Christian Doctrine of Apokatastasis*, 724–38.

Gregory of Nyssa

Gregory of Nyssa was even more definite and comprehensive in his doctrine of *apokatastasis* than Origen. Nyssa is one of the very great fathers of the church and he has never been condemned for his position on *apokatastasis.* There are many treatments available of Nyssa's teaching on *apokatastasis*. I choose that of Ludlow because she is a specialist in the thought of Nyssa; later we shall consider Rahner's position on the topic.

Gregory's Arguments for Universal Salvation

From the Nature of Evil (Quotes within the text are from Gregory)

"The nature of evil will pass over to non-existence, having been made to disappear completely by being, and the divine and unmixed goodness will contain all rational nature within itself; for nothing which came into being through God will fall short of God's kingdom. When all evil which is mixed with beings . . . has been released through the refinery of purifying fire, everything which had its being through God will be such as it was from the beginning, when it never received evil."

This claim, which Gregory makes in his commentary on 1 Cor 15: 28, is based on that verse's assertion that "when all things are subject to him, then the Son himself will also be subjected to him who put all things under him, that God may be all in all."

Clearly . . . Paul asserts the unreality of evil . . . in saying that God who is everything to each thing will be in everything. For indeed it is not when something evil is left in beings, or, if it is truly necessary to believe that he will be in everything, the existence of nothing evil is demonstrated together with this belief about him.

Coupled with the premise that God is totally and infinitely good (a theme that runs throughout Gregory's theology) and the logical premise that the perfect good can in no way be in anything evil, this assertion that God will be in everything thus proves to Gregory's satisfaction that there will be no evil left.

One is still faced, however, with the question of whether God *will* in fact be in everything. Ultimately, Gregory relies on Scripture for his certainty on this point; nevertheless a Neoplatonic concept of evil does strengthen his assertions. Gregory believes that "to be in evil is, properly speaking, not to be, since evil itself has no existence on its own but the non-existence of good gives rise to evil. It will pass away and disappear at the proper times, when the universe is restored to the good, so that no trace of the evil which now prevails over us remains in the life which lies before us in hope."

However, Gregory seems only to show that evil is liable to cease existing, not that it will do so necessarily.[10]

Argument from the Unity of Humanity

First, humanity was created as a whole. Gregory appears to think that the image of God is to be found specifically in humanity as a unity; consequently, he seems to be committed to asserting that the image will be restored in humanity as a whole, when the resurrection brings the restoration of the image: "I do not doubt that there will be one race of all people when we will all be one body of Christ, shaped in one form, when the divine image will shine out in all equally."

Secondly, there is involved in the concept of the unity of humanity the notion that a specific number of souls make up the human race: "His end is one, and only one, it is this: when the complete whole of our race shall have been perfected from the first man to the last . . . to offer to every one of us participation in the blessings which are in Him."

The clear implication is that the transformation can only occur when every soul has come to life, because every soul must be transformed.

Thirdly, one version of this argument seems to be that, by the very nature of the salvation he effected Christ saved the whole human race, not certain members of it. Christ's body is the whole human race. Because humanity was created as a whole, it will be resurrected as a whole.[11]

Augustine

With Augustine we reach a new and longlasting turning point in the history of *apokatastasis* in Christian tradition. I turn again to Ramelli as she is perhaps one of the most authoritative scholars on Augustine's views on this subject.

10. Ludlow, *Universal Salvation*, 86–87.

11. Ibid., 89–90.

Here I shall limit myself to reconstructing Augustine's repudiation of the doctrine of *apokatastasis,* which he had embraced in the years of his polemic against Manichaeism, and to suggesting possible cause for this repudiation.

Contrary to the Alexandrian school, Augustine stated that God's purpose in the creation of this world was not the purification of the fallen rational creatures. He argued that *ignis aeternus* must mean "eternal fire," or else the righteous' bliss could not be eternal. Origen, however, demonstrated that eternal life and eternal death cannot subsist together, since they are two contradictories.

The imprecision of the Latin vocabulary of eternity can help to explain Augustine's argument. While, as I have often mentioned, the bible describes as *aidios* only life in the world to come, thus declaring it to be "eternal," it never describes as *aidia* punishment, death, and fire applied to human beings in the world to come; these are only and consistently called *aiovia*, "belonging to the future eon." But in Latin both adjectives are rendered with one and the same adjective, *aeternus* (or *sempiternus),* and their distinction was completely lost.

This, of course, had important consequences on the development of the doctrine of *apokatastasis.* That Augustine was utterly unaware of the difference between the two Greek adjectives and the relevant implication is clear. Augustine, just as many Latin authors, was unable to grasp this distinction. Augustine dubbed the supporters of the *apokatastasis* doctrine *misericords,* describing them as "those merciful Christians who refuse to believe that infernal punishments will be *eternal*." Origen is depicted as "the most merciful of all" because of his doctrine of the eventual restoration of the devil.

However, even after abandoning the doctrine of *apokatastasis* himself, Augustine very interestingly recognised that a great deal of Christians in his day did embrace it, "indeed the vast majority." These very numerous Christians, "albeit not denying the Holy Scripture, do not believe in eternal torments."

Augustine himself was convinced, like Origen, that divine grace is necessary for humans to be saved, but from his point of view God's grace is destined to only a group of human beings out of a *massa damnationis,* while Origen thought it to apply to all human beings, in addition to all other rational creatures.[12]

12. Ramelli, *Apokatastasis,* 669–76.

Balthasar on Augustine

Quoting Walter Kasper: "Neither Holy Scripture nor the church's Tradition of faith asserts with certainty of any man that he is actually in hell. Hell is always held before our eyes as a *real possibility*, one connected with the offer of conversion and life."[13]

> I found that the transformation of this "real possibility" into "objective certainty" occurred with the great church Father Augustine, whose opinion (whether traceable back to his ten years of Manichaeism may be left open here) has cast an enormous shadow over the history of Western theology, to the extent that the biblical warnings against taking our ultimate fate lightly have been transformed—indeed actually vitiated—into information about the outcome of the judgment by God that awaits us.[14]

And Balthasar quotes approvingly from one André Manaranche:

> But God predestines no one to hell. The limitation of the great Saint Augustine is found at that point where he throws sacred history out of balance by centering it on Adam instead of Christ. [His conception of] judgment is oriented on the first fall, in the absence of the coming Redeemer to whom God will hand over the whole of judgment. How does Augustine know that there are men who are damned? God has revealed nothing of the sort to us, has given us no list of names. Jesus teaches us only, but clearly and plainly, indeed ardently and persistently, that damnation is possible, that we have to fear it, especially we, his friends, who are in danger of betraying him. Augustine, however, has damned the whole world in Christ. He is no better informed about hell than is Origen, who puts no one in there. But how does he [Augustine] know that?[15]

Hebrew Thought Compared with Greek

It is a common opinion that Augustine did not know Greek, or did not know it very well (as Ramelli points out). Thus he didn't know either too much about the difference between Greek and Hebrew thinking. This is

13. Balthasar, *Dare We Hope*, 164.

14. Ibid., 165.

15. Ibid., 72

another approach to a resolution of this question of the meaning of "eternal" as the Lord uses it in his parables.

In a section entitled "The Israelite Conception of Time," Boman has this to say: "The commonest word for boundless time is *olam*. Since *olam* means only an unbounded time, in certain contexts it can encompass a period relatively short according to our objective way of thinking; thus a bondsman is one who can *never* obtain his freedom (Deut 15:17); or again, he serves his master *forever* (Exod 21:6)."

Although in the Old Testament *olam* always means time which is boundless in a certain respect, nothing is said therein of the objective duration of astronomical time; it is always the concern of exegesis to ask in each case how far the authors gaze pursues time."[16]

Another fruitful line of thought concerns the meaning of "duration" in the two languages. For the Greeks it means something that goes on and on and on. But "in the Semitic languages the notion of recurrence coincides with that of duration. Thus *odh* means first the return of something, then its recurrence, and this idea passes over into duration. Human life runs its course as an eternal rhythm—earth man—rhythm. They thought of the circular course as an eternal rhythm of beginning, continuation, and return to the beginning."[17]

I am aware that these brief quotes from this very important book are very frustrating and do not resolve the meaning of "eternal" in the Gospels. I simply mention this linguistic difference as another avenue to pursue about this question. We are Greeks, and we tend to read the words of the Gospels as Greeks. But Jesus, of course, had a Hebrew mind. It`s possible that an in-depth study of this book could help to resolve this problem of the meaning of "eternal."

John the Scot Eriugena (d. 877)

Eriugena is little known to most Christians, but he is a towering figure in the Western Christian tradition. Part of his uniqueness is that he knew Greek and translated some of the early Greek classics (e.g., Dionysius the Areopagite) into Latin. But more importantly for our topic, it means he could read the Alexandrine tradition of Origen and his followers, especially Gregory of Nyssa. Because of this he was a firm believer in *apokatastasis*

16. Boman, *Hebrew Thought*, 152–53.

17. *Ibid., 134*.

when it was practically unknown and considered heretical because of Augustine. He ascribes Augustine's errors regarding *apokatastasis* to his ignorance of Greek. (I don't know what he was teaching at the time, but the poor guy was stabbed to death by his students!) I turn once again to Ramelli.

> In Nyssen, Eriugena found "traces of eschatology that was orientated to *apokatastasis*." God predestined no one to damnation, but only to eternal salvation. For evil and the relevant punishment do not subsist ontologically; therefore they cannot be foreseen and predestined. Since evil is an ontological negation, the suffering of other worldly punishment will be the absence of beatitude and, as Nyssen taught, will have no physical place. What is punished is not one's ontological nature, but one's sinning will.
>
> The torment itself is called by Eriugena an *occultissima operatio*, that is, a mysterious operation of God's providence, since thanks to it the final *reditus [return]* of sinners to God will take place. Even demons will be reintegrated into the perfect totality in the end, when creation will coincide once again with its eternal model, the product of God's creative knowledge, in which all realities subsist from all eternity. All creatures will experience the aforementioned *reditus*, which, in turn, in its universality, is to be considered a universal *apokatastasis*. There is no rational creature who does not want to escape misery and attain happiness. This set of ideas clearly points to the final reintegration of sinners.
>
> The death of the body is the death of death, and the beginning of *apokatastasis*. Eriugena describes the stages: the first is the dissolution of the body and its return to the four elements; the second will be the resurrection of this same body; the third, its transformation into a spiritual body; the fourth, the return of the whole human nature to its primordial causes in God, that is, God's Ideas; the fifth, the return to the whole nature, together with its primordial cause (the ideas), to God, so that God will be "all in all." This is the *telos* described according to I Cor 15: 28, the favorite passage of Origen and Nyssen in support of *apokatastasis*.
>
> It is also very clear that *apokatastasis* for Eriugena, just as for Origen and Nyssen, depends on Christ, an incarnated Christ who is also a cosmic Christ, the Logos, who has assumed every creature in itself. Eriugena insists on the assumption of humanity as a whole and the unity of all in Christ, when humans will be like angels because Christ has unified the human race, and the divine nature in himself. Eriugena observes that God's Logos does not deliver any human being to eternal punishment since human beings are

creatures of God. God will be not only in few or in many but in all, absolutely, once both evil and death have vanished altogether.

Eriugena, who read Greek, knew that in this [Matt 25:41] and similar passages Scripture employs *aionios* and not *aidios*, a distinction that was completely blurred in Latin, with the translation of both with *aeternus*. From the ontological point of view, only God is eternal, and torments could never be coeternal with God.

Eriugena's *theoriae* review the whole range of the history of salvation: the first is the original condition of the human being, wanted by God; the second is the historical existence of each single human being in this world; the third is the return of all humanity to its angelic state; the fourth is, not only the restoration, but also the deification of human beings, and the fifth—which comes even after deification—is the contemplation of all the goods that God's generosity will bestow on all.[18]

By way of conclusion: The Main Features of the Christian *Apokatastasis* Theory from the New Testament to Eriugena, and Its Theological Significance.

The doctrine of *apokatastasis*, as is found, from the New Testament to Eriugena, in many Christian texts and Patristic authors, is a Christian doctrine and is grounded in Christ. Indeed, the Christian doctrine of *apokatastasis* is based on the incarnation, death, and resurrection of Christ and on God's being the supreme Good. It is also founded upon God's grace, which will "bestow mercy upon all," and the divine will—which these patristic authors saw as revealed by Scripture—"that all humans be saved and reach the knowledge of Truth." They also considered it to be revealed in Scripture, and in particular in a prophecy by St. Paul, that in the *telos*, when all the powers of evil and death will be annihilated, and all enemies will submit (for Origen and his followers, in a voluntary submission), "God will be all in all." The *apokatastasis* doctrine is historically very far from having been produced by an isolated character, excessively influenced or even "contaminated" by Greek theories, such as Origen has been long considered to be. The *apokatastasis* doctrine is embedded in a much broader tradition, which is rooted in the New Testament itself and, even back, in some Jewish universalistic expectations, as I have argued.

Origen and his followers considered the doctrine of *apokatastasis* to be grounded, much more than in Greek philosophy, in the Bible and especially in the New Testament. The doctrine of

18. Ramelli, *Apokatastasis*, 782–816.

apokatastasis as the eventual universal salvation is an authentically Christian, or Jewish-Christian doctrine. Before Christianity, no religion or philosophy had ever maintained it, not even Plato or mystery religions.

Another fundamental characteristic of Patristic *apokatastasis* is—what at first might sound paradoxical—its orthodoxy. In fact, the main Patristic supporters of this theory, Origen and Gregory of Nyssa, did support it in defense of Christian "orthodoxy," against those which were regarded as the most dangerous heresies of their time. I have shown that up to the end of the fourth century many Christians adhered to this doctrine. It is meaningful that all of the Patristic supporters of *apokatastasis* were faithful to the Christian church; among them many saints.[19]

Ludlow

The intention of this chapter has been neither to provide an exhaustive account of all those people who have advocated universal salvation, nor to defend any particular belief by recourse to a close examination of the traditional doctrines of the church. Rather, my aim has been to show not only that there has been a more or less continuous tradition of universalism within (and on the penumbra of) Christianity, but also that there has been a side variety of universalist beliefs. So often, a belief in universal salvation is taken to be a uniform thing, motivated by one or two narrow theological aims: on the contrary, this chapter reveals the diversity of contexts and motivations which have contributed to different universalist views. The debate over universalism is thus broader than a simple opposition of "Origenist" and "Augustinian" theologies. It is also broader than merely the question of whether all will be saved, for it inevitably raises the questions "how?" and "why?" Nevertheless, what is also striking is that most of the writers I have examined, despite their many speculations, have ultimately based their convictions on the biblical promises that God wills all to be saved and that in the end, God will be all in all.[20]

19. Ibid., 617–18, 823.

20. Ludlow, "Universalism," 215.

Daley

Another disputed point, at the end of the Patristic age and beyond, was the actual *extent of eschatological salvation.* Origen's clear hope for the salvation of all spiritual creatures—the *apokatastasis penton*—was shared openly by Gregory of Nyssa and Evagrius, as well as by some sixth century anti-Chalcedonian writers, but bitterly contested by others from Origen's time onward. Jerome, even after his repudiation of Origen in 394, continued to argue that at least all Christian believers will experience the final mercy of God. Augustine assumed, on the other side, that the majority of human beings will not be saved and that even the perseverance of believers in the life of grace is far from assured. Both positions have found their passionate defenders throughout Christian history, and continue to be proposed in our own time. Both remain enshrouded in the double, mutually limiting mystery of God's providential love and the genuineness of human freedom.[21]

21. Daley, *Hope*, 222.

— 3 —
Modern History

The Protestant Tradition: Pre-Twentieth Century

Friedrich Schleiermacher (1768–1834)

Schleiermacher is a towering figure in Protestant theology, often called "the Father of Modern Theology." He is frequently cited in discussions on universalism.

Parry and Partridge

Friedrich Schleiermacher was the first really prominent influential theologian since the Patristic period to consider universalism. He had doubts about the traditional notion of hell from a young age, and when he was a mature scholar asked in a journal whether the doctrine of the eternal punishment of sinners could fit with this "eternal fatherly love of God."

In an appendix on the subject in *The Christian Faith* he argues that the biblical evidence for eternal damnation is inconclusive and challenges the coherence of the idea of an eternal punishment: if the punishment was physical it simply could not go on for ever, he asserts, and if it consisted of the pains of conscience "we cannot imagine how the awakened conscience, as a living movement of the spirit, could fail to issue in some good."

His assumption is that good punishment is reformatory, bringing with it "a sharpened feeling for the difference between good and evil." Eternal punishment would render the state of the blessed imperfect, whether they were aware of hell or not (for Schleiermacher, ignorance would not be bliss.)

Therefore Schleiermacher suggests that one should admit the force of the "milder view that through the power of redemption there will be one day a universal redemption of all souls." This is, however, by no means a forceful and absolute defence of universalism, and elsewhere in *The Christian Faith* Schleiermacher is cautious about making statements about the concept of judgment and the afterlife.

It is important, nevertheless, that he steers away from a notion of universalism which involves the idea of the "sudden recovery of all souls for the Kingdom of Grace" after death, and sees the process of reformative punishment after death in parallel with "the complete purification of the soul due to the appearance of Christ" and a growing "receptivity for the knowledge of Christ."

There is much here that reminds one of Origen (whom Schleiermacher occasionally cites) and Gregory of Nyssa. Schleiermacher's views on eternal punishment influenced the ideas of some of his pupils and universalism continued to attract attention throughout the heyday of German liberal Protestantism.[1]

John Hick

Schleiermacher figures prominently in Hick as he examines mostly the great theologian's views about the theme of evil and the God of love. But at the end he comments about Schleiermacher's eschatology. Quotes within the text are from Schleiermacher. Hick writes:

> In his eschatology, dealing with the other end of the creative process, Schleiermacher rejects the gratuitous increment to the problem of evil that is proposed by Augustine and Calvinist doctrine of double predestination—the predestining of some to a joyous fellowship with God and others to eternal torment.
>
> Indeed, "no divine fore-ordination can be admitted as a result of which the individual would be lost to fellowship with Christ. Thus we may reasonably persist in holding this single divine fore-ordination to blessedness." And so at the end of a long and complex discussion of the notion of a double destiny (in heaven and hell) he rejects the Augustinian and Calvinist doctrine of eternal damnation

1. Parry and Partridge, *Universal Salvation?*, 207–8.

and concludes, undogmatically, in favour of the eventual universal efficacy of Christ's redeeming work. He points out that perpetual torment could not coexist with the bliss of heaven, for,

"Even if externally the two realms were quite separate, yet so high of degree of bliss is not as such compatible with entire ignorance of others' misery, the more so if the separation itself is the result purely of a general judgment, at which both sides were present, which means conscious of each other. Now if we attribute to the blessed a knowledge of the state of the damned, it cannot be a knowledge unmixed with sympathy. If the perfecting of our nature is not to move backwards, sympathy must be such as to embrace the whole human race, and when extended to the damned must of necessity be a disturbing element in bliss, all the more that, unlike similar feelings in this life, it is untouched by hope."

And again from Schleiermacher:

> "From whichever side we view it, then, there are great difficulties in thinking that the finite issue of redemption is such that some thereby obtain highest bliss, while others (on the ordinary view, indeed the majority of the human race) are lost in irrevocable misery. We ought not to retain such an idea without decisive testimony to the fact that it was this that Christ Himself looked forward; and such testimony is wholly lacking. Hence we ought at least to admit that through the power of redemption there will one day be a universal restoration of all souls."[2]

Powys

I will try to give a brief summary of Powys's article. My purpose in including this section is to supply a brief history of my theme during the nineteenth and twentieth centuries, as well as to emphasize that the questions now being debated among Christians are not new, but were publicly and exhaustively discussed over 150 years ago in the English speaking theological world (to which I confine my research). The quotes are all from Powys.

The nineteenth and early twentieth century saw a wide-ranging debate on the questions of "unending punishment, conditional immortality and universal salvation," especially in the Church of England. "Reformation theology was as firmly grounded in retributive concepts as pre-Reformation thought." The debate was initiated "on account of the dominant

2. Hick, *Evil*, 240–41.

philosophical themes of the value of the individual and the expectation of progress." The central question was, as always, how can a God of love condemn anyone to eternal pain?

"The predominant and orthodox position during the Middle, Reformation and post-Reformation Ages was that the fate of the unrighteous was to suffer unending physical punishment." How to get around this position?

Responses varied: 1) the pain is remedial and will eventually cease. This bothered many since it could logically lead to universal salvation; 2) God will destroy the person turned against him: conditional immortality; 3) universalism. "The Church of England had left the matter of universalism an open question." Another common position was that decisions for or against God did not end with death but people had an opportunity after death to continue to change and be converted. The position of one of those involved in the debates, W. R. Alger, is representative of one of the major trends:

> Alger too attacked the traditional doctrine, and set himself the task in the latter part of his massive work "to disprove the popular dogma which asserts that the state of the condemned departed is a state of *complete damnation absolutely eternal* [emphasis original]. The substance of his attack is to be found chiefly in an appeal to an interpretation of the doctrine of Christ's descent to hell, and in his contention that an irreversible punitive fate would be unjust, "incompatible with any worthy idea of the character of God" and inconceivable. Such a challenge was in full accord with the mood of the age. It provided an attractive marriage of belief in the immortality of the soul and belief in ongoing progress. It was this provision . . . that made the path to universalism the more attractive to the Victorians.
>
> By 1938, at least within the Church of England, the view that the divine purpose regarding the unrighteous as merely punitive had "as an inference from the Christian doctrine of God as a whole" come to be largely abandoned.
>
> It would seem that much of the energy that has gone into the nineteenth and twentieth century debates about hell and universalism may have been wasted on account of the undue influence of unjustified presuppositions. The waste has arguably been compounded by the way in which the debate has been constrained by a pervasive though perverse allegiance to a questionable "orthodoxy": the doctrine of immediate, unending, physical punishment.[3]

3. Powys, "The Nineteenth and Twentieth Centuries," 93–138; emphasis original.

John G. Adams

Powys's article deals mostly with the movement of universalism in England. Adams's book is exclusively concerned with the movement in America: "What is written for these pages will represent especially the rise and progress of the Universalist Church in America. It is proper, however, to say that the faith it represents has had growth also in other lands. It has long been known in Great Britain, where a few churches have made a distinct avowal of it."

You may be as surprised as I was of the extent of the teaching of universalism in America in the latter part of the nineteenth century. Adams's book is mostly a catalogue of the ministers and congregations who believed in this teaching. There is no need to present names and churches here. My purpose is to briefly make you aware that there was such a universalist movement in America. I quote from the author's summary of the doctrine generally taught in these New England congregations.

> If the Fatherhood of God, the brotherhood of the race, the unceasing obligation of man to love God and his fellow-creatures, the lordship and mission of Christ the Saviour of the world, *the immortality of all mankind* [emphasis added], are not positive doctrines of the New Testament, then no doctrines, no precepts, no principles can be proved from it. This is the very question at issue between Universalists and those who deny that their faith has its foundations in the New Testament.
>
> As the Lord liveth, the now "open questions" will one day be settled, and settled on the side of the divine Beneficence. The love of God in Christ has come into the world, and will not go out of it until its work is here done; love that is long suffering, that rejoiceth not in iniquity, but rejoiceth in the truth; that beareth, believeth, hopeth and endureth all things, and that never faileth; love that will bring *the last lost one home, that will obliterate all the hells, and people all the heavens in the universe.* [emphasis added][4]

4. Adams, *Fifty Notable Years*, 247, 253–54.

4

Twentieth-Century Catholic Authors

The Second Vatican Council

In Deak's survey of the twentieth century he only finds a few Catholic authors who, as he put it, made some daring searches for new ways other than the predominant dualistic approach of most Catholic theologians; but they

> did not tackle the entire problematic of universalism. They became involved in the discussion mainly because they proposed alternative solutions to the heretofore prevailing (but essentially ailing) theories and doctrines.
>
> When we consider the essential virtue of a Catholic theologian not to rely exclusively on the bible, and especially not to rely exclusively on his own interpretation, but also on the live directives supplied by the teaching office of the church, then, in the twentieth century, the Second Vatican Council should be considered *the* authority representing the direction for the entire Catholic Church.
>
> However, by examining the documents of this council, we can be justifiably surprised, for they do not at all reflect the traditional features of a dualistic eschatology. The terms, such as "hell," "condemnation," "eternal torments," "eternal punishment" (and all their synonyms) do not occur in any document of this Council, whether pastoral or dogmatic. The idea of last judgment appears only twice.
>
> Chapter VII of the Dogmatic Constitution on the Church, which bears the original title "On the Eschatological Nature of the Pilgrim Church and its Union with the Heavenly Church" would

> have been the proper place to elaborate the doctrine of hell to some extent. Instead we see nothing more than an enumeration of ten Bible quotations placed side by side with almost no text in between. To our understanding this attitude of Vatican II means not only that the traditional doctrine of hell is far from being a "fundamental doctrine of the Catholic Church," but also that instead it experiences a period of reflection and re-examination with the endorsement of the council itself.
>
> For those New Testament passages this document quotes, have to be in harmony with *any* orthodox eschatological doctrine. The vital question lies on the right interpretation of these texts, which the council did not intend to fix at this time, but has rather left open as a future task of biblical and systematic theology.[1]

The Catholic theology texts on the last things seminarians would have used before the Council would pretty much have been along dualistic lines. They were for me. The Catholic writers we will now consider reflect the searching for *new approaches* to eschatology the Council encouraged by its silence. Their thinking began *before* the Council.

Teilhard de Chardin

In a section where the author presents some modern theories regarding *apokatastasis,* he gives first place to Teilhard de Chardin. As you will see, Teilhard is agnostic in his position. The quotes are from the *Divine Milieu.*

> In the year 1926–27, Pierre Teilhard de Chardin (d. 1955) wrote: "Of the mysteries which we have to believe, O Lord, there is none, without doubt, which so affronts our human views as that of damnation . . . You have told me, O God, to believe in hell." In this formulation, one feels the strain a person must undergo to reconcile God's love and mercy with the possibility of eternal rejection or damnation. Teilhard was evidently able to reconcile both realities only through an act of obedience. This obedience is evident in his words: "O Jesus, closing my eyes to what my human weakness cannot as yet understand and therefore cannot bear—that is to say, to the reality of the damned—I desire at least to make the ever present threat of the damned a part of my habitual and practical vision of the world." In the spirit of obedience, Teilhard also felt himself supported by ecclesiastical teaching, and practice. After he confessed that God had commanded belief in hell, he adds: "But

1. Deak, *Apokatastasis,* 336–37.

> you have forbidden me to hold with absolute certainty that any single man has been damned. I shall therefore make no attempt to consider the damned here nor even to discover–by whatever means–whether there are any."

In connection with this matter of "belief in hell," the author quotes von Balthasar: "There remains a serious question: Can supernatural faith—faith as personal surrender—be directed toward instances of calamity? In the ecclesiastical confession of faith there are only facts of salvation."[2]

Edith Stein (St. Benedicta of the Cross) 1891–1942

Edith Stein was a fine philosopher before she became a Catholic, and she continued to write and study as a Carmelite nun. I don't know the date of the following excerpts from her writings: it is quoted by Balthasar in a kind of summary of his reflections on universalism; and this indicates the importance he gave to her views. It concerns mostly the question of human freedom in relationship to divine freedom. One of the common arguments against any kind of final universalism is that the human person is always free, and therefore it is always possible to say no to God's invitations. (I will deal with this issue more extensively below.) From Edith Stein:

> We attempted to understand what part freedom plays in the work of redemption. For this it is not adequate if one focuses on freedom alone. One must investigate as well what grace can do and whether even for it there is an absolute limit. This we have already seen: grace must come to man. By its own power, it can, at best, come up to his door but never force its way inside. And further: it can come to him without his seeking it, without his desiring it. The question is whether it can complete its work without his cooperation.
>
> It seemed to us that this question had to be answered negatively. That is a weighty thing to say. For it obviously implies that God's freedom, which we call omnipotence, meets with a limit in human freedom. Grace is the Spirit of God, who descends to the soul of man. It can find no abode there if it is not freely taken in. That is a hard truth. It implies—besides the aforementioned limit to divine omnipotence—the possibility, in principle, of excluding oneself from redemption and the kingdom of grace.
>
> It does *not* imply a limit to divine mercy. For even if we cannot close our minds to the fact that temporal death comes for

2. Ambaum, *An Empty Hell?*, 42–43, 46.

countless men without their ever having looked eternity in the eye and without salvation's ever having become a problem for them; that, furthermore, many men occupy themselves with salvation for a lifetime without responding to grace—we still do not know whether the decisive hour might not come for all of these somewhere in the next world, and faith can tell us that this is the case.

All-merciful love can thus descend to everyone. We believe that it does so. And now, can we assume that there are souls that remain perpetually closed to such love? As a possibility in principle, this cannot be rejected. *In reality*, it can become infinitely improbable—precisely through what preparatory grace is capable of effecting in the souls. It can do no more than knock at the door, and there are souls that already open themselves to it upon hearing this unobtrusive call.

Others allow it to go unheeded. Then it can steal its way into souls and begin to spread itself out there more and more. The greater the area becomes that grace thus occupies in an illegitimate way, the more improbable it becomes that the soul will remain closed to it. For now the soul already sees the world in the light of grace. It perceives the holy whenever it encounters this and feels itself attracted by it. Likewise, it notices the unholy and is repulsed by it; and everything else pales before these qualities.

To this corresponds a tendency within itself to behave according to its own *reason* and no longer to that of nature or the evil one. If it follows this inner prompting, then it subjects itself implicitly to the rule of grace. It is possible that it will not do this. Then it has need of an activity of its own that is directed against the influence of grace. And this engaging of freedom implies a tension that increases proportionately the more that preparatory grace has spread itself through the soul. This defensive activity is based—like all free acts—on a foundation that differs in nature from itself, such as natural impulses that are still effective in the soul alongside grace.

The more that grace wins ground from the things that had filled the soul before it, the more it repels the effects of the acts directed against it. And to this process of displacement there are, in principle, no limits. If all the impulses opposed to the spirit of light have been expelled from the soul, then any free decision against this has become infinitely improbable. Then faith in the unboundedness of divine love and grace also justifies *hope for the universality of redemption*, although, through the possibility of resistance to grace that remains open in principle, the possibility of eternal damnation also persists.

Seen in this way, what were described earlier as limits to divine omnipotence are also canceled out again. They exist only as long as we oppose divine and human freedom to each other and fail to consider the sphere that forms the basis of human freedom. Human freedom can be neither broken nor neutralized by divine freedom, but it may well be, so to speak, outwitted. The descent of grace to the human soul is a free act of divine love. And there are no *limits* to how far it may extend. Which particular means it chooses for effecting itself, why it strives to win one soul and lets another strive to win it, whether and how and when it is also active in places where our eyes perceive no effects—those are all questions that escape rational penetration.

For us, there is only knowledge of the possibilities in principle and, on the basis of those possibilities in principle, an understanding of the facts that are accessible to us.[3]

Ludlow: Karl Rahner's View of Universalism.

Gregory of Nyssa declares his expectation [of the salvation of all] with certainty while Rahner is content merely to express a hope. Rahner does not set out a formal argument for universal salvation. This brings one to the issue of his hermeneutics and in particular his hermeneutics of eschatological assertions. This is the nearest he comes to a formal argument for the truth of universal salvation.

Because human freedom, and in particular of human freedom to say no to God, hell is a possibility for *all* people. Furthermore, because of the complex and elusive nature of human decision, one cannot make pronouncements (at least during someone's lifetime) about whether other people have escaped that possibility. One cannot even be absolutely sure that one is not a sinner oneself. However, although hell is a possibility for all, one is not required to believe that any people have, in fact, been damned. In addition, it is certain, in light of the salvific work of Christ, that at least some have been saved (for example, saints and martyrs) and at a general level, one can be sure that God's grace will be effective. Thus it is possible that all will be saved: indeed Christians should hope for this outcome, based on the revelation of the victorious grace of Christ which brings the world to its fulfillment.

3. Quoted in Balthasar, *Dare We Hope?*, 218–21.

Consequently, one cannot avoid speaking of both heaven and hell, but these two outcomes are not to be regarded in precisely the same light: as Rahner expresses it, they are not parallel.

This view is usually expressed by Rahner in terms of a hope (that all will gain heaven) and a possibility (that some may go to hell). For example, his claim that the words of Christ about hell are "threat discourses" follows the principle that scriptural statements about hell express only a possibility for each human, not an actuality for some. Similarly, he does not usually appear to take 1Corinthians 15:28 to mean that, necessarily, each individual will be saved, but seems to treat it as an expression of God's will for the whole world which the Christian hopes will be fulfilled.

However, occasionally (and particularly in his later writings) he makes a blunter assertion which is seemingly a paradox. For example, in *Foundations of Christian Faith* he writes: "The existence of the possibility that freedom will end in eternal loss stands alongside the doctrine that the world and the history of the world as a whole will *in fact* enter into eternal life with God." (Italics in text) Here the second, apparently universalistic, claim is expressed in terms which go beyond hope.[4]

St John Paul II

The following excerpts of St. John Paul II are from a variety of papal documents—encyclicals, general audiences, post-synodal exhortations, messages to religious orders, and homilies. It is not necessary here to try and give each of these its proper dogmatic value. It is generally agreed that the encyclical has the highest, but even here we are not speaking of any kind of infallible statement. Popes also are entitled to theologumena, although, admittedly, they carry more weight than those of ordinary theologians.

Thus, the reader may give her or his own interpretation to the following statements the Pope made about "universal salvation." By presenting these citations I don't mean to imply that the Pope means by "universal salvation" what Gregory of Nyssa meant. Nevertheless, it is significant that the Pope uses "universal salvation" and similar phrases. His reflections are simply offered as part of the discussion we are having.

> Eternal damnation remains a possibility, but we are not granted, without a special divine revelation, the knowledge of whether or

4. Ludlow, *Universal Salvation*, 244–45.

which human beings are effectively involved in it. (General Audience—July 28, 1999)

Christ, Redeemer of man, now for ever "clad in a robe dipped in blood" (Apoc 19, 13), the everlasting, invincible guarantee of universal salvation. [Message of John Paul II to the Abbess General of the Order of the Most Holy Saviour of St. Bridget]

If the Holy Spirit, the Paraclete, is to convince the world precisely of this "judgment," undoubtedly he does so to continue Christ's work aimed at universal salvation. We can therefore conclude that in bearing witness to Christ, the Paraclete is an assiduous (though invisible) advocate and defender of the work of salvation, and of all those engaged in this work. He is also the guarantor of the definitive triumph over sin and over the world subjected to sin, in order to free it from sin and introduce it into the way of salvation. [General Audience—May 24, 1989]

[The church] is all the more serviceable for her mission of salvation *for* all: God "desires all men to be saved and to come to the knowledge of the truth." Accordingly, what is in question here is man in all his truth, in his full magnitude. We are not dealing with the "abstract" man, but with the real, "concrete," "historical" man. We are dealing with "each" man, for each man is included in the mystery of the Redemption and with each one Christ has united himself for ever through this mystery.

The Second Vatican Council points out this very fact when, speaking of that likeness, it recalls that "man is the only creature on earth that God willed for itself." Man as "willed" by God, as "chosen" by him from eternity and called, destined for grace and glory—this is "each" man, "the most concrete" man, "the most real"; this is man in all the fullness of the mystery in which he has become a sharer in Jesus Christ, and the mystery in which each one of the four thousand million human beings living on our planet has become a sharer from the moment he is conceived beneath the heart of his mother. [Encyclical *Redemptor Hominis*, 5, 13]

"Blessed be the God and Father of our Lord Jesus Christ, who has blessed us in Christ with every spiritual blessing in the heavenly places" (Eph 1:3). These words of the Letter to the Ephesians reveal the eternal design of God the Father, his plan of man's salvation in Christ. It is a universal plan, which concerns all men and women created in the image and likeness of God (cf. Gen 1:26). Just as all are included in the creative work of God "in the beginning," *so all are eternally included in the divine plan of salvation, which is to be completely revealed, in the fullness of time,* with the final coming of Christ. In fact, the God who is the "Father of our Lord Jesus

Christ"—these are the next words of the same Letter—"chose us in him before the foundation of the world, that we should be holy and blameless before him. *He destined us in love* to be his sons through Jesus Christ, according to the purpose of his will, to the praise of his glorious grace, which he freely bestowed on us in the Beloved. In him we have redemption through his blood, the forgiveness of our trespasses, according to the riches of his grace" (Eph 1:4-7). [Encyclical, *Redemptoris Mater,* 7:1; emphasis original]

The church's universal mission is born of faith in Jesus Christ, as I stated in our Trinitarian profession of faith: "I believe in one Lord, Jesus Christ, the only Son of God, eternally begotten of the Father . . . For us men and for our salvation he came down from heaven: by the power of the Holy Spirit he became incarnate from the Virgin Mary, and was made man." The redemption event brings salvation to all, "for each one is included in the mystery of the redemption and with each one Christ has united himself forever through this mystery." Just as "by his incarnation the Son of God united himself in some sense with every human being," so too "we are obliged to hold that the Holy Spirit offers everyone the possibility of sharing in the Paschal Mystery in a manner known to God." God's plan is "to unite all things in Christ, things in heaven and things on earth" (Eph. 1:10). It is necessary to keep these two truths together, namely, the real possibility of salvation in Christ for all mankind and the necessity of the church for salvation. We know, however, that Jesus came to bring integral salvation, one which embraces the whole person and all mankind, and opens up the wondrous prospect of divine filiation. Why mission? Because to us, as to St. Paul, "this grace was given, to preach to the Gentiles the unsearchable riches of Christ" (Eph 3:8). Newness of life in him is the "Good News" for men and women of every age: all are called to it and destined for it. [Encyclical, *Redemptoris Missio,* 4, 6, 9, 11]

In proclaiming the Risen Lord, Christians present the One who inaugurates a new era of history and announce to the world the good news of a complete and universal salvation which contain in itself the pledge of a new world in which pain and injustice will give way to joy and beauty. At the beginning of a new millennium marked by a clearer awareness of the universality of salvation and a realization that the Gospel daily needs to be proclaimed anew, the Synodal Assembly raised an appeal that our commitment to mission should not be lessened but rather expanded, through ever more profound missionary cooperation. [Post-Synodal Apostolic Exhortation *Pastores Gregis*]

This affirmation of the Saviour's "uniqueness" derives from the Lord's own words. He stated that he came "to give his own life in ransom for the many" (Mk 10:45), that is, for humanity, as St. Paul explains when he writes: "One died for all" (2 Cor 5:14; cf. Rom 5:18). Christ won universal salvation with the gift of his own life. No other mediator has been established by God as Savior. The unique value of the sacrifice of the cross must always be acknowledged in the destiny of every man. For those, however, who have not received the Gospel proclamation, as I wrote in the Encyclical *Redemptoris Missio*, salvation is accessible in mysterious ways, inasmuch as divine grace is granted to them by virtue of Christ's redeeming sacrifice, without external membership in the church, but nonetheless always in relation to her (cf. RM 10). It is a mysterious relationship. It is mysterious for those who receive the grace, because they do not know the church and sometimes even outwardly reject her. In order to take effect, saving grace requires acceptance, cooperation, a yes to the divine gift. This acceptance is, at least implicitly, orientated to Christ and the church. Religions can exercise a positive influence on the destiny of those who belong to them and follow their guidance in a sincere spirit. The church does not exist nor does she work for herself, but is at the service of a humanity called to divine sonship in Christ (cf. RM 19). She thus exercises an implicit mediation also with regard to those who do not know the Gospel. [All Salvation Comes Through Christ. General Audience—May 31, 1995]

Journeying through the centuries, reliving every day the Sacrifice of the altar, the church, the People of God, awaits Christ's coming in glory. This is proclaimed after the consecration by the Eucharistic assembly gathered around the altar. Time after time with renewed faith the church repeats her desire for the final encounter with the One who comes to bring his plan of universal salvation to completion. [Message of His Holiness John Paul II for the World Mission Sunday 2004: "Eucharist and Mission"]

This universal mission of salvation takes on great importance on the day when the church commemorates the conversion of St. Paul. Among the Apostles, in fact, Paul himself expresses and fulfills the church's universal mission in a particular way. On the road to Damascus Christ associates him with the divine plan of universal salvation: "The God of our fathers appointed you to know his will, for you will be a witness for him to all men of what you have seen and heard" (Acts 22:14-16). [Homily During the Mass with His Holiness Aram I as Part of Week of Prayer for Christian Unity, Saturday, 25, January, 1997]

St. Paul underscored this salvific value in regard to Christ's obedience. If sin came into the world through an act of disobedience, universal salvation was obtained by the Redeemer's obedience: "For as by one man's disobedience many we were made sinners, so by one man's obedience many will be made righteous" (Rom 5:19). [Religious Offer Their Own Wills to God. General Audience—December 7, 1994]

As we read again in the council, to achieve universal salvation, Christ sent from the Father his Holy Spirit, who was to carry on inwardly his saving work and prompt the church to spread out (AG). [The Church is Missionary by Her nature. General Audience—April 19, 1995]

St. John Paul II, *Crossing the Threshold of Hope*

In Christ, God revealed to the world that He desires "everyone to be saved and to come to the knowledge of the truth" (1 Tim 2:4). This phrase from the first Letter to Timothy is of fundamental importance for understanding and preaching the Last Things. If God desires this—if, for this reason, God has given His Son, who in turn is at work in the church through the Holy Spirit—*can man be damned*, can he be rejected by God?

The problem of hell has always disturbed great thinkers in the church, beginning with Origen and continuing in our time with Mikhail [Sergius] Bulgakov and Hans Urs von Balthasar. In point of fact, the ancient councils rejected the theory of the "final *apokatastasis,*" according to which the world would be regenerated after destruction, and every creature would be saved; a theory which indirectly abolished hell. But the problem remains. Can God, who has loved man so much, permit the man who rejects Him to be condemned to eternal torment? And yet, the words of Christ are unequivocal. In Matthew's Gospel He speaks clearly of those who will go to eternal punishment (cf. Mt 25:46). Who will these be? The church has never made any pronouncement in this regard.

This is a mystery truly inscrutable, which embraces the holiness of God and the conscience of man. The silence of the church is, therefore, the only appropriate position for the Christian faith. Even when Jesus says of Judas, the traitor, "It would be better for that man if he had never been born," (Mt 26:24), His words do not allude for certain to eternal damnation.

At the same time, however, there is something in man's moral conscience itself that rebels against any loss of this conviction: Is not God who is Love also ultimate Justice? Can He tolerate these terrible crimes, can they go unpunished? Isn't final punishment in some way necessary in order to re-establish moral equilibrium in the complex history of humanity? Is not hell in a certain sense the ultimate safeguard of man's moral conscience?

The Holy Scriptures includes the concept of the *purifying fire.* The Eastern Church adopted it because it was biblical, while not receiving the Catholic doctrine on purgatory.

Besides the Bull of Benedict XII from the fourteenth century, the mystical works of St. John of the Cross offered me a very strong argument for purgatory. The "living flame of love," of which Saint John speaks, is above all a purifying fire. The mystical nights described by this great Doctor of the church on the basis of his own experience corresponds, in a certain sense, to purgatory. God makes man pass through such an interior purgatory of his sensual and spiritual nature in order to bring him into union with Himself. Here we do not find ourselves before a mere tribunal. We present ourselves before the power of Love itself.

Before all else, it is Love that judges. God, who is Love, judges through love. It is Love that demands purification, before man can be made ready for that union with God which is his ultimate vocation and destiny.

Perhaps this is enough. Many theologians, in the East and West, including contemporary theologians, have devoted their studies to the Last Things. The church still has its eschatological awareness. It still leans man to eternal life. If the church should cease to do so, it would cease being faithful to its vocation, to the New Covenant, which God has made with it in Jesus Christ.[5]

Hans Urs von Balthasar.

Balthasar is considered to be one of the greatest Catholic minds of the twentieth century, perhaps the greatest. He was made a cardinal by St. John Paul II but died before he could receive the red hat. (The Pope said he had gone to a higher reward!) His book, *Dare We Hope That All Men be Saved?*, has never received any kind of official *monitum* (warning) from the Vatican.

5. St. John Paul II, *Crossing the Threshold of Hope*, 185–87.

Balthasar gives his response to most of the objections to such a hope. As mentioned in my Preface, not all theologians in the church agreed with him. He received some very severe criticisms about this view and his opinion on this matter still receives objections. Of course he was not infallible, but anyone who disagrees with him must have some very substantial theological and philosophical credentials. His opinion will continue to carry an extraordinary weight in the Catholic Church, and hopefully continue to make the hope for universal salvation more of a permanent part of Christian consciousness.

One of the best, very short presentations of *Dare We Hope?* is by Mark Brumley, the president and CEO of Ignatius Press, which published the book. I offer here only a few of his comments most relevant to my theme.

> Let me cut to the theological chase: the Swiss theologian Hans Urs von Balthasar wasn't a Universalist. Not if a *Universalist* is one who claims for certain all men will be saved. Or, to put it differently, that no one—including ourselves—will be lost. This side of eternity, according to Balthasar, we simply can't know, either way, whether all people will be saved or whether "two eternal outcomes"—one of salvation and one of damnation—will be realized. Whatever Balthasar's position is, and whether or not it is correct, it isn't universalism.
>
> Right now, we stand under judgment; the outcome isn't determined and there is the real possibility of damnation, not just for others but for ourselves as well. We have *hope*, not certainty, of salvation for all, Balthasar maintained. Nor did he see such hope as inconsistent with missionary work—just the opposite. The Christian must care about the salvation of others as well as his own salvation; he must be an agent, by grace, of salvation for others and in this way for himself as well.
>
> Balthasar unhesitatingly affirmed the Bible's warning about damnation. But he saw *two sets* of biblical texts: (1) the *two outcomes* passages (Heaven and Hell) and (2) *the salvation of all* passages. In Balthasar's view, which set of biblical texts will ultimately be realized depends on how, exactly, human history plays out. Because we can't be certain which way things will turn out, Balthasar argued, we shouldn't write off anybody as inevitably damned, nor should we presume everybody will be saved (including ourselves). We must heed the warning of the "two outcome" set of texts while hoping (and working) for the goal of the "salvation of all" texts.
>
> Of course just because Balthasar was no Universalist doesn't mean he is beyond criticism or his exegesis is correct.

All theologians are subject to critique; that's part of the theology business. But many of Balthasar's critics, in order to portray him as a Universalist, simply neglect or minimize, or paint as disingenuous, the repeated and clear statements he made about the real possibility of damnation. They also often fail to appreciate the severe, unfair attacks he encountered, and they don't take these into proper consideration when reading his responses.

The fact is, Balthasar didn't say we're all guaranteed heaven. *Hoping* for all to be saved certainly doesn't excuse anyone from evangelizing. When we ask Jesus to "lead all souls to heaven, especially those most in need of his mercy," as we pray at the end of each decade of the Rosary, do we exempt ourselves and others from evangelizing? Why shouldn't hoping, praying, and working for the salvation of all be among the means by which God realizes such universal salvation?[6]

Maurice Blondel

What I offer here from *Dare We Hope?* is a commentary on the views of Maurice Blondel on universalism that I have not found in other books. Balthasar entitles this section, "Blondel's Dilemma."

Blondel was one of the most outstanding Catholic philosophers of modern times (1861–1947). One chapter in *Dare We Hope?* deals with his struggle with the "problem of hell." I chose to summarize this chapter to show that prominent Catholic philosophers have also been preoccupied with the question of universalism. Balthasar especially chose to consider Blondel's views about hell because "through his *L'Action* (1893) he gave Catholic thought a decisive new beginning—struggled with the problem of an everlasting hell." Blondel speaks of hell as a "possible consequence, with the church never, after all, having officially linked it to any particular person."

Blondel "acquits" God of responsibility for eternal damnation: "The guilty one hates and accuses himself. Thus hell has not been created by God; it is the logical and moral consequence of the sin of the guilty."

Then Balthasar gets into the heart of Blondel's dilemma, which he contends Blondel never resolved—"a bitter but nevertheless seemingly undecided struggle." Basically it's the question of God's freedom versus man's freedom.

6. Brumley, *Dare We Hope.*

In Blondel's master work, *L'Action,* he says that "action is a synthesis of man and God; neither God alone nor man alone can change, produce or destroy it." Earlier, in his diaries, he wrote that man's choice can turn out negatively, "containing in itself the sin against the Holy Spirit that is unpardonable in the next world." Blondel accepts that self-damnation is a possibility. He accepts this "because the doctrine of eternal damnation (based on the age-old tradition stemming from Augustine and the Middle Ages) appears to him as an unassailable reality."

Nonetheless, Balthasar sees that Blondel comes close to his, Balthasar's, own position of hope:

> Thus Blondel struggles through to a conclusion. Blondel loves to make the point that man should not pass judgment but should show mercy toward all sinners. His reason for this is that God has reserved justice for him and left mercy up to us.
>
> But his formulation remains one-sided: "You have entrusted [to man] the task of mercy, have presented him with your life, your fruitfulness, your omnipotence for the sake of goodness only; you have reserved justice for yourself. Thus we, too, are obliged to love sinners, since mercy, in order that it be even more strongly contrasted with vengeful justice, has been incarnated in us and for us. We should be less intent than God upon justice. Nevertheless, mercy grows on the sternness of justice. Do not shrink from extending the divine perfections. Each one increases them all."[7]

Mercy over Justice

One of the main questions concerning universalism is: "If God is all just, how can he allow the unrepentant to go without punishment; if he is all merciful, how can he deny salvation to sinners despite their resistance?" A frequent answer is that his justice and mercy is the same thing (Barth, MacDonald). At the conclusion of the main text of his book Balthasar gives a different response to this question that I have not found in other authors: God's mercy and goodness are *greater than his justice.*

> But between the misdeeds of the creature and the goodness of God there is no equilibrium, which means that justice with respect to the former is subordinated to divine mercy, indeed, must be virtually a mode of this mercy. That such things as man and world exist

7. Balthasar, *Dare We Hope?*, 114–24.

at all is by no means due to God's justice but solely to his goodness, and it is not until God's bottomless generosity designs to create something non-divine that viewpoints such as "justice, generosity and mercy" arise and become relevant.

Insofar as God bestows upon creatures what they deserve, he is just; insofar as he bestows it upon them not for the sake of his own advantage but purely out of goodness, and insofar as the perfections bestowed upon things by God overcome anything defective, he acts mercifully.

We can look at this in a more detailed way: to each is owed what he is entitled to, and on the basis, in fact, of an inner necessity. In the created being, this debt can extend in two directions: for one, toward other created things (thus the part is directed toward the whole, and every created thing toward its end); but then, too, every created thing is directed toward God. Here, then, we can speak of a twofold indebtedness: God owed the created being whatever is in accordance with his wisdom and will and, given that, whatever his goodness allows to become manifest; in this sense, God's justice is an expression of what befits himself, through which he guarantees himself what he owes himself.

On the other hand, he owes the created being whatever befits that being, for instance, in the case of man, that he has hands or that the animals are subject to him. *But this sort of indebtedness is dependent upon the first.* For if God gives a created being what is owed, that does not mean that he himself is a debtor, since, after all, he is not ordered toward his creatures, but they are ordered toward him.

That they exist at all, and are what they are, is due not to God's justice but solely to his goodness and generosity, which means that his justice—in respect of both himself and his creatures—is to be seen as a mode of his goodness. "The work of divine justice always presupposes the work of mercy and is grounded in it." A being can be owed something only on the basis of something that exists in advance: a man is owed hands because he possesses a rational soul; he possesses that, however, because he is a man, and since the chain cannot extend to infinity, the final link is: the man owes himself, as such, solely to divine goodness. "Thus, in each of God's works, his mercy appears as the primary root," and because first causes persist most strongly in the effects, therefore, "God, from the superabundance of his goodness, gives more generously to the creature than is demanded for that creature's inner stability. For less would suffice for the preservation of the order of justice than is actually granted by divine goodness, which exceeds every internal creaturely relationship."[8]

Comments in the following article fit in with Balthasar's reflections above concerning mercy over justice.

Given human nature, it is not surprising that the issues of justice that arise regarding the doctrine of hell have received much more attention than those surrounding the doctrine of heaven. Most of us are more comfortable getting benefits we do not deserve or gifts that are inappropriate than we are shouldering burdens that are not ours or suffering pain we do not deserve.

The fundamental point to notice here, however, is that the doctrines of heaven and hell are not separable in this way. They are intimately linked, and the account one accepts of one constrains the kind of account one can develop of the other. These points may seem obvious, but they are ignored regularly, especially in discussions of the nature of hell. If we think of hell as a place of punishment, the logical contrast would seem to indicate that heaven is a place of reward. Yet, the Christian conception denies that heaven is fundamentally a reward for faithful service; it is, rather, the free and gracious gift of a loving God, unmerited by anything we have done.

Another way to put this tension is to note that explanations of why some go to heaven and others go to hell seem to have little in common. On the usual position, admission to heaven is explained in terms of God's love, not his justice or fairness, whereas consignment to hell is explained in terms of his justice rather than his love. Such explanations are at best incomplete, for love and justice often pull us in different directions regarding how to treat people. Some ways of treating people are just, but unloving; and some ways are caring, but less than just. At the very least, some explanation is required concerning the interaction of the motives God has in establishing heaven and hell.

More can be said, however. In the Christian view, God's fundamental motive must be conceived in terms of love rather than justice. Justice has no hope of explaining the two great acts of God, creation and redemption; only love can account for them. If so, however, one's account of hell ought to accord with this

8. Ibid., 154–56.

hierarchical conception of God's motivational structure as well. In particular, it will not do to portray God as fundamentally loving until we reach the point of discussing the nature of hell, and suddenly portray God as fundamentally a just God.[9]

Peter Phan

Peter Phan is one of the foremost Catholic scholars writing on eschatology in the United States. His book on Rahner's eschatology won the Best Book Award from the College of Theology Society in 1989. I have already used some of his reflections in this *Guide*. Here I first present his specific treatment of *apokatastasis* in Rahner. (Although we have already seen some of Rahner's views on this topic, Phan presents some additional insights.)

After giving a brief account of *apokatastasis* in the tradition, Rahner's position on the "serious possibility of eternal loss," and the serious obstacles to universal salvation such as human freedom and the mystery of the acceptance or non-acceptance of God's grace, Phan states Rahner's specific position. Quotes within the text are from Rahner.

> Precisely because eternal hell is such an absolute self-contradiction, Rahner often reminds his readers that eternal salvation and eternal perdition are not two parallel choices. The Christian faith, he points out, professes that the world and the human race as a whole will *in fact* enter into eternal life with God. Heartened by this conviction, Rahner wonders whether the ancient doctrine of *apokatastasis*, although condemned by the church, can be rehabilitated in an acceptable way.
>
> On the other hand, to deny a priori the *possibility of apocatastasis* would be to impose arbitrary limits upon the supreme sovereignty of God's will. Human freedom is embraced by God's more powerful freedom and mercy. Although there is in the Scripture no theory of an *apokatastasis*, and although no affirmation is possible on the *theoretical* plane that the antecedent will of God is in fact such that it establishes final salvation for the individual, nevertheless it is possible to hope for an *apokatastasis*. "There is nothing to prevent a Christian's hoping (not knowing) that in practice the final fate of every human being, as a result of the exercise of his or her freedom by the power of God's grace, which dwarf's and also redeems all evil, will be such that hell will not in the end exist. Christians may

9. Kvanvig, "Hell," 420–21.

> have this hope (first for others and therefore also for themselves) if, within their histories of freedom, they seriously consider the opposite: final damnation. In having to consider this, Christians are doubtless doing something essential to Christian existence."
>
> The doctrine of *apokatastasis* is then indissolubly linked with the theology of hope. Humanity encounters God's saving will not in theoretical certainty but in hope. But we can never tell ourselves with certainty whether we are really hoping except by *hoping*, that is, by taking refuge in what is beyond our control. For Rahner, hope is not a transient mode or provisional form of faith and charity but a prior medium or common factor between knowledge and will, between faith and love. Further, it is the virtue of hope that makes *apokatastasis* an acceptable and orthodox doctrine. Faith, Rahner points out, can only proclaim God's universal salvific will as a *general* principle. This faith as such cannot tell me as an *individual* whether God has conferred efficacious grace precisely on *me* in particular and in thus bringing about my salvation in the concrete.
>
> "Hope, then," says Rahner, "is the act in which we base ourselves beyond our power to control, namely, upon God who, in himself, can be the God of grace or the God of anger, but who in this case is apprehended as the God of grace and under no other aspect." Hope, in this sense, is not a mere consequence of faith; the basis for such hope is not something that faith can provide, but rather something that is grasped solely by hope as such.
>
> But if this hope for salvation is possible for me as an individual, there is no reason why it should not be extended to others, and indeed to all beings. On the contrary, Rahner argues, it is the Christian's duty to extend it first to others and then to one self. Hence, the doctrine of *apocatastasis* is justified by the virtue of hope, not as a statement of fact, but as an object of hope and prayer.[10]

In his "Critical Questions" after the above treatment of Rahner's position, Phan says this:

> Finally, hell as an eternal punishment does not seem on the one hand to be compatible with God's omnipotence and infinite love; on the other hand, if one says that hell is not imposed by God but created by human freedom, hell with its absoluteness does not appear to be a proportionate product of that fragile and precarious freedom.

10. Phan, *Eternity in Time*, 77–81.

> One cannot but admire and concur with Rahner's attempt to overcome these objections by placing the Christian discourse on hell within the context of Christ's definitive victory, of the absolute validity of human freedom, and of the importance of Christian hope. Nevertheless, one may wonder whether the scarce attention and space Rahner has dedicated to sin and hell, on the one hand, and, on the other, the strong emphasis he placed on the certainty of the salvation of the world *as a whole* as well as his speculation on *apocatastasis* (even only as an object of hope) do not lead one to make light of the threat of eternal self-loss. His repeated protests against the number of the damned and his insistence on our ignorance of whether anyone will actually be lost at all may ironically produce another surreptitious calculation that affirms that there is and there will be no one in hell. Barth has expressed the issue with particular vigor: "The church will not then preach an *apocatastasis,* nor will it preach a powerless grace of Jesus Christ or a wickedness of men which is too powerful for it. But without any weakening of the contrast, and also without any arbitrary dualism, it will preach the overwhelming power of weakness of human wickedness in face of it." Has Rahner preserved this delicate balance?[11]

Nine years later, in a question-and-answer style, Phan basically gives the same Rahnerian position:

> According to Rahner, we know, on a *general or theoretical level,* that God wills to save *all* human beings. Whether, in the *concrete*, as applied to *me,* this universal salvific will will in fact be efficacious or not, I cannot say with certainty. I can only hope that it will be so. And since I may and must hope that I will be saved, I may and *must* extend that hope to others, even first to others and only then to myself. So says Rahner:
>
> "There is nothing to prevent a Christian's hoping (not knowing) that in practice the final state of every human being, as a result of the exercise of his or her freedom by the power of God's grace, which dwarfs and also redeems all evil, will be such that hell will not exist in the end. Christians may have this hope (first for others and therefore also for themselves) if, within their histories of freedom, they seriously consider the opposite: final damnation."[12]

11. Ibid., 152–58.

12. Phan, *Responses to 101 Questions*, 87–88.

John R. Sachs, SJ

We have already seen Sachs as regards the history of *apokatastasis.* I give here some of his general comments from an earlier article, and some of his conclusions. He covers most of the issues we have been discussing, using Balthasar and Rahner frequently for his argumentation.

> How could a loving God create a world in which human freedom has the capacity to damn itself eternally? . . . At the same time the Church has refused to assert that anyone in fact had died or will die in such a state [of mortal sin at death] . . . Thus heaven and hell are not to be considered equally possible outcomes, either for humanity as a whole or for individual human beings . . . Both Balthasar and Rahner have insisted that the human "yes" and "no" to God are not on the same level. Human freedom is simply and most radically the capacity for God, not the capacity for *either* God *or* something else. . . .
>
> [About judgment:] But what about the nature of God's judgment? If there were nothing more to final judgment than the finalizing of our own "fundamental option," if that event were nothing more than the divine declaration that what we have freely made of our life will be so for eternity, if the process of Christian dying were nothing more than a "freezing" of what we have already accomplished (or failed to accomplish!), then the gospel would hardly be good news and we should approach death and judgment with horror. But strictly speaking, God's final judgment can only be the final future fullness of God's forgiving, life-giving judgment in the cross and resurrection of Christ. It cannot be merely a neutral "taking stock"; it is an expression of God's real victory over sin and death, in which anything and everything which has been done in love is saved and perfected by God.

His conclusions:

> We have seen that there is a clear consensus among Catholic theologians today in their treatment of the notion of apocatastasis and the problem of hell. Christian faith proclaims the reality of the universal salvation revealed and accomplished by God in the death and resurrection of Christ. The real possibility of hell is understood by most to be an expression of the Christian belief in the ultimate seriousness and responsibility of the freedom which God has endowed humanity. God's offer must be freely accepted; no one can be saved against his or her will.

A properly Christian universalism emphasizes that God wills salvation for all men and women and somehow effectively offers it to them, even where there is no explicit knowledge of Christ or belief in God. It may not be said that only a preordained number will be saved, and certainly not that some are preordained to be damned. Likewise, it may not be said that even one person is already or will in fact be damned. All that may and must be believed is that the salvation of the world is a reality already begun and established in Christ.

Finally, a doctrine concerning the obligation to hope for the salvation of all has an important ethical imperative: we must truly live what we hope for. Thus the hope about which we have been speaking is not merely a hope that all will be restored at some final point, but that already here and now, all men and women are being saved. This hope, then, demands a certain posture not only with respect to future fulfillment, but to present life. Do I live here and now as one who hopes that all are being saved?[13]

The Linn Brothers

The authors of this book are Dennis and Matthew Linn and Sheila Fabricant Linn. In the 70s and 80s the Linn Brothers were very prominent in the charismatic healing movement in the Catholic Church. I met them. We have seen that one of the driving theological thrusts behind the eschatology of universalism is the terrible image of God that an eternal hell fosters. As part of their attempt, therefore, in their retreats, to healing our image of God, questions about hell invariably arose in the question and answer periods after their conferences. We will see that the Linn Brothers were quite aware of some of the trends we are briefly documenting in this *Guide.* I present these question-and-answer exchanges to show that the opinions regarding *apokatastasis* in this *Guide* are becoming fairly common currency in our Catholic teachings.

Q. What do you mean when you say that hell exists as a possibility?

A. Given what we know of the loving nature of God, we may have real hope that God will actually save everyone.

13. Sachs, "Current Eschatology," 217, 239, 251, 252–53.

> **Q.** What about saints and other mystics who claim to have seen people burning in the fires of hell?
>
> **A.** Just as we cannot take all the images in scripture literally, neither can we take all the images in visions (such as fire and hell) literally.
>
> **Q.** You sound awfully optimistic. Are other people in the church really saying the same thing?
>
> **A.** Rahner argues for an "unshakable hope" that in the end all men and women will be healed and will enjoy eternal life.[14]

Other questions were the common ones we have seen during our present inquiry: What about Paul's harsh sayings? What about the Lazarus parable? What about the idea that we make a final decision at the moment of death? What about the parable of the goats and sheep? It is not necessary to go into the answers of the Linn Brothers to these common objections except to emphasize that their answers correspond basically to the general theology in this *Guide*. They even quote many of the same authors.

Zachary Hayes

In this very small book only three pages are devoted to universalism. There is nothing in it that we have not already seen. I reference it as an example of what was probably the majority opinion of Catholic theologians in the latter part of the twentieth century and may still be the majority view today. Hayes sees that one of the major problems for universalism is how to reconcile it with human freedom. He refers to Robinson (below) and Hick whom we have seen. He quotes Hick: "As faith looks to the future, it becomes a faith in the universal triumph of the divine love."

> While one cannot deny that this argument has a certain appeal, it labors under weaknesses similar to those in Robinson's argument. Both see the dilemma to be between freedom and coercion. But is this the real point at issue? Is it not rather the question whether a human person can really and finally reject love? Human experience offers evidence of people who seem quite capable of doing

14. Linn, *Good Goats*, 66–67.

this, though no one can make any final judgment about such people. Furthermore, the Universalist position seems incapable of accepting the idea that in creating the kind of world he has created, God has made himself really dependent on the historical response of his creatures in working out his intention. Neither Robinson nor Hick has offered a convincing solution to the problem of human freedom. It remains an open question whether it is possible to combine human freedom with some form of universalism.[15]

Leo Scheffczyk

Fr. Scheffczyk is a Polish Catholic theologian. I include this excerpt to show that there is an ongoing discussion within Catholicism about universalism. Scheffczyk emphasizes the double realities of heaven and hell and thinks that those proposing unversalism do not have the proper faith conviction about hell. However, at the end of his article he admits the final answers lie in the mystery of God: "In the face of this mystery only the stance of humility and reverence is seemly for man in the face of the inscrutable."[16] Here is some of his critique of universalism:

> It cannot be denied that the thought of the reconciliation of all exercises a great power of appeal to contemporary feelings. Here the drama of the world becomes a resplendent *apotheosis* of the victorious God (despite the stress on the radical seriousness of decision-making for human existence). Dissonances in the world's course are resolved in a harmonious chord, a pure sound pleasing to human ears. The unity of a humanity which has survived trials is raised to the highest solidarity in salvation.
>
> But on the level of theological rationality, one also must see the shadowy side which increases this fascination. One will recognize that wherever the teaching on universal reconciliation is directly advocated, the difficulties of responsible belief become immense. One cannot change orthodoxy on this single point and replace the dual outcome of human history by a simple end. Whoever abandons this position must also abandon or radically alter many basic tenets of faith. Whoever agrees to *apocatastasis* can maintain belief in a final judgment only in an extremely attenuated sense in which condemnation is possible (if at all) "in time" or "with confirmation."

15. Hayes, *What Are They Saying?*, 59.

16. Scheffczyk, *Apocatastasis*, 397.

> He can no longer believe in the finality of otherworldy conditions (the sinner must be able—not without his own activity—to accomplish holiness even in the next life). The death of human beings loses the decisive character of the end of the *status viae*, because even after death the way to salvation is still open. Life thus loses its unique critical pregnancy. The redemption by Jesus Christ, from whom all salvation originates, is seen not only with regard to its objective adequacy, but also with regard to its subjective efficacy as universal and comprehensive. Objective and subjective redemption practically unite, but with that the thought of the necessity of human development is altered, just as the mystery of the gratuity of grace and election by God are altered. Finally, the teaching on *apocatastasis* even goes against the concept of God, because the God who would overlook the firmly rooted evil of the sinner and so really affirm it, must end by denying himself.[17]

Ralph Martin.

I decided to mention this book even though the author himself does not accept universalism. He does, however, attest to its growing acceptance among Catholics since Balthasar's book. I would highly recommend especially his chapter 6: it is a good refutation of Balthasar's thesis from a Catholic point of view. It would be important reading concerning the traditional view in the light of modern universalist opinions my *Guide* is attempting to make better known. Martin sees universalist views as undermining the church's call to evangelization. Even though this call is clearly in the church's documents, he argues that it has not been sufficiently heeded:

> Perhaps the reason why these strong calls to evangelization which do, in a secondary way, mention elements of the "biblical worldview" concerning sin, error, and the work of the devil, were not able to counter successfully the undermining currents is that the arguments from authority is not a strong argument for ordinary human beings. The reasons for the command—namely, that the eternal destinies of human beings are really at stake and for most people the preaching of the gospel can make a life-or-death, heaven or hell difference—need to be unashamedly stated.
>
> This is certainly why Jesus often spoke of the eternal consequences of not accepting his teaching—being lost forever, hell—and did not just give the command to evangelize. This is why Mark

17. Ibid., 395–96.

> 16:16, which is referenced in *Lumen Gentium* 16 but not directly quoted, makes explicit that what is at stake is being "saved" or "condemned." Jesus makes it clear Christianity is not a game or an optional enrichment opportunity but a precious and urgent opportunity to find salvation and escape damnation. In fidelity to the teaching of Christ this is what motivated two thousand years of heroic missionary work and the heroic witness of countless martyrs.[18]

Martin's conclusion—although he does not put it this way—comes down to accepting that the ideas of people eternally in hell and that God is love can and should be reconciled in the Christian mind:

> A major cluster of Balthasar's pastoral concerns revolves around preserving a good image for God. Indeed, many people have very distorted understandings of God, ranging from God as an unpredictable, moralistic, judgement tyrant, to a permissive, affirming, symbolic image of our own goodness and divinity. The only good image of what God is like is by his own revelation of himself to us. Attempts to correct a particular distorted image of God can, unfortunately, end up by creating a distortion in the opposite direction.
>
> The image of God that emerges from the tradition's reflection on one of the bible's major themes, the "two ways, two choices, two destinations," is capable of producing a profound, holy, and spiritually and psychologically healthy fear of God, disposing one for the deepest and most intimate gift of loving union. Both fear and love are necessary.
>
> Balthasar's pastoral concern that people who believe in a populated hell will fail in charity is not well founded; the opposite appears to be the case.[19]

Fr. Robert Barron

Barron is well known for his video series *Catholicism*. He has been in dialogue with Martin about his book.

> Now the heart of Martin's book is a detailed study and critique of the theories of Rahner and Balthasar, and space prevents me from even sketching his complex argument. I will mention only one dimension of it, namely his analysis of Lumen Gentium paragraph 16. Both Balthasar and Rahner—as well as their myriad

18. Martin, *Will Many Be Saved?*, 204.

19. Ibid., 189–90.

disciples—found justification in the first part of that paragraph, wherein the Vatican II fathers do indeed teach that non-Christians, even non-believers, can be saved as long as they "try in their actions to do God's will as they know it through the dictates of their conscience."

However, Martin points out that the defenders of universal salvation have, almost without exception, overlooked the next section of that paragraph, in which the Council Fathers say these decidedly less comforting words: "But very often, deceived by the Evil One, men have become vain in their reasonings, have exchanged the truth of God for a lie, and served the world rather than the Creator. Hence to procure the salvation of all these the church . . . takes zealous care to foster the missions." A fair reading of the entire paragraph, therefore, would seem to yield the following: the unevangelized can be saved, but often (*ut saepius*), they do not meet the requirements for salvation. They will, then, be damned without hearing the announcement of the gospel and coming to an active faith.

I found [Martin's] central argument undermined by one of his own footnotes. In a note buried on page 284 of his text, Martin cites some remarks of Pope Benedict XVI that have contributed, in his judgment, to a confusion on the point in question. He is referring to observations in sections 45–47 of the Pope's encyclical *Spe Salvi,* which can be summarized as follows: There are a relative handful of truly wicked persons in whom the love of God and neighbor has been totally extinguished through sin, and there are a relative handful of people whose lives are utterly pure, completely given over to the demands of love. Those latter few will proceed, upon death, directly to heaven, and those former few will, upon death, enter the state that the church calls Hell.

But the Pope concludes that "the great majority of people" who, though sinners still retain a fundamental ordering to God, can and will be brought to heaven after the necessary purification of Purgatory. Martin knows that the Pope stands athwart the position he has taken throughout his study, for he says, casually enough, "The argument of this book would suggest a need for clarification."[20]

20. Barron, "Response." Also, cf. below 87–89 in *Spe Salvi.*

Martin's reply to Fr. Robert Barron

My point is to reveal the urgency of evangelization—to invite people who may currently be on the broad way leading to destruction, to leave it and find the source of life, Christ and the church. People who may be on the broad way don't need to stay on it and I think more Catholics will be willing to take the risk to "give a reason for the hope that is within them" if they realize that something ultimate is really at stake—heaven or hell.

All I am claiming, with Vatican II is that "very often" people find themselves in a perilous situation regarding salvation and we can't presume they will be saved without coming to explicit faith, repentance and baptism.[21]

Does Universalism Deemphasize Evangelization?

Kronen and Reitan

Others may worry that if we embrace the doctrine of universalism, the Christian call to evangelism becomes pointless. If all are saved then the urgency to spread the gospel is lost—but there are several reasons to think this worry misplaced.

First, Christian universalists generally think there are positive life benefits (in terms of life satisfaction and resources for moral improvement) that are possible *in this life* if (and only if) one opens oneself up to the kind of relationship with God that Christianity claims has been made available through Christ's life and work. Desiring that others enjoy these benefits *here and now* would be a motive to evangelize.

Secondly, one might believe that while universal salvation is inevitable, this is not because there is no subjective requirement for salvation but because all will *eventually* meet this requirement. If so, enjoying union with God is only possible for those who have opened themselves up to it—and while it is certain that all will eventually do so, those who do not by the time of their death will exist after death in a state of alienation from God that can only bring increasing misery the longer it lasts. The efforts of human evangelists may be one of God's means for hastening the salvation of all, with Christians called to be God's agents in this way. In the absence of human evangelical efforts, more people might

21. Martin, "Renewal," 348.

experience the finite "hell" of alienation from God for longer before realizing their error and turning to God.

Third, Christian Universalists might be convinced the Christian worldview makes the most sense of human experience, fitting its elements together into the most coherent whole as well as offering pragmatic resources for living better lives. In other words, one might be convinced Christianity is the worldview most likely to be true. In this case, one might be motivated to share the Christian world view for the same reason that Richard Dawkins preaches atheism—a belief that one has the truth (or at least the most rational worldview) combined with the belief that it is good in itself if more people believe the truth.

Finally, and we think most significantly, "evangelist" means "good messenger" and evangelism is not primarily about conversion and salvation but about declaring good news as widely as possible. In this sense the motivation for evangelism is, at least in part, the same sort of motivation that would impel someone to call everyone they knew as soon as they learn that their child has been cured of leukemia. They want to share their joy at this wonderful news; but in the case of the Christian gospel, the news also seems to have beneficial pragmatic implications for those it is being shared with. If people are hunkering down in their cellars waiting for enemy planes to fly overhead and drop bombs, the news that the enemy has been defeated will mean that people can come out of their hidey-holes. In such a case, running through the streets shouting out the good news is not merely motivated by a desire to share a personal joy but to let people know that they no longer need to burden themselves in a particular set of ways.[22]

Pope Benedict XVI and *Spe Salvi*

What does Pope Benedict's encyclical *Spe Salvi* contribute to the discussion about universalism? And, secondly, because Balthasar's book on universalism is a major influence in this *Guide,* the question also arises: What was the influence, if any, of *Dare We Hope?* on the Pope's encyclical? I don't have any documentation, but I will simply presume that Benedict read this book. Balthasar guided Ratzinger's doctrinal studies, and was one of his mentors. In keeping with the plan of this *Guide,* I will simply present the most relevant passages of *Spe Salvi* as part of our ongoing reflections.

22. Kronen and Reitan, *God's Final Victory*, 183–84.

46. For the great majority of people—we may suppose—there remains in the depths of their being an ultimate interior openness to truth, to love, to God. In the concrete choices of life, however, it is covered over by ever new compromises with evil—much filth covers purity, but the thirst for purity remains and it still constantly re-emerges from all that is base and remains present in the soul. What happens to such individuals when they appear before the Judge? Will all the impurity they have amassed through life suddenly cease to matter? What else might occur? Saint Paul, in his First Letter to the Corinthians, gives us an idea of the differing impact of God's judgment according to each person's particular circumstances. He does this using images which in some way try to express the invisible, without it being possible for us to conceptualize these images—simply because we can neither see into the world beyond death nor do we have any experience of it. Paul begins by saying that Christian life is built upon a common foundation: Jesus Christ. This foundation endures. If we have stood firm on this foundation and built our life upon it, we know that it cannot be taken away from us even in death. Then Paul continues: "Now if any one builds on the foundation with gold, silver, precious stones, wood, hay, straw—each man's work will become manifest; for the Day will disclose it, because it will be revealed with fire, and the fire will test what sort of work each one has done. If the work which any man has built on the foundation survives, he will receive a reward. If any man's work is burned up, he will suffer loss, though he himself will be saved, but only as through fire" (1 Cor 3:12–15). In this text, it is in any case evident that our salvation can take different forms, that some of what is built may be burned down, that in order to be saved we personally have to pass through "fire" so as to become fully open to receiving God and able to take our place at the table of the eternal marriage-feast.

47. Some recent theologians are of the opinion that the fire which both burns and saves is Christ himself, the Judge and Saviour. The encounter with him is the decisive act of judgment. Before his gaze all falsehood melts away. This encounter with him, as it burns us, transforms and frees us, allowing us to become truly ourselves. All that we build during our lives can prove to be mere straw, pure bluster, and it collapses. Yet in the pain of this encounter, when the impurity and sickness of our lives become evident to us, there lies salvation. His gaze, the touch of his heart heals us through an undeniably painful transformation "as through fire." But it is a blessed pain, in which the holy power of his love sears through us like a flame, enabling us to become totally ourselves and thus

totally of God. In this way the inter-relation between justice and grace also becomes clear: the way we live our lives is not immaterial, but our defilement does not stain us for ever if we have at least continued to reach out towards Christ, towards truth and towards love. Indeed, it has already been burned away through Christ's Passion. At the moment of judgment we experience and we absorb the overwhelming power of his love over all the evil in the world and in ourselves. The pain of love becomes our salvation and our joy. It is clear that we cannot calculate the "duration" of this transforming burning in terms of the chronological measurements of this world. The transforming "moment" of this encounter eludes earthly time-reckoning—it is the heart's time, it is the time of "passage" to communion with God in the Body of Christ The judgment of God is hope, both because it is justice and because it is grace. If it were merely grace, making all earthly things cease to matter, God would still owe us an answer to the question about justice—the crucial question that we ask of history and of God. If it were merely justice, in the end it could bring only fear to us all. The incarnation of God in Christ has so closely linked the two together—judgment and grace—that justice is firmly established: we all work out our salvation "with fear and trembling" (Phil 2:12). Nevertheless grace allows us all to hope, and to go trustfully to meet the Judge whom we know as our "advocate," or *parakletos* (cf. 1 John 2:1).[23]

Richard John Neuhaus. *Will All Be Saved?*

Richard John Neuhaus was the founder of *First Things* magazine and one of the most articulate and influential Catholic intellectuals of the twentieth century in the United States. Here are some of his comments at the time when Balthasar's book was being discussed.

> We may come at our question in a different way by trying this thought experiment: Do you know anyone of whom you would *not* say that you hope he or she is saved? Imagine that you could know everyone who now lives, who has ever lived, or will live in the future. Of whom could you say that you hope they are eternally damned? Perhaps in a fit of anger—or in an act of presumption in which you identified your moral indignation with God's

23. www.vatican.va/holyfather/benedictxvi/encyclicals.

perfect justice—you have said that you hope somebody is eternally damned, but you know you were wrong in saying or thinking that. "Forgive us our sins, as we forgive those who sin against us." Is it possible to forgive someone and, at the same time, hope he goes to hell? I think not. After you have, in this thought experiment, said to absolutely everybody, "I hope you will be saved," have you not declared your hope that all will be saved?

Quite apart from such a thought experiment, the fact is that we all pray that all men be saved. Is it possible to pray for that without hoping for that? I think not. It follows that we pray, and therefore we hope, that all will be saved. Catholics by the millions pray the rosary every day, adding at the end of each decade, *O my Jesus, forgive us our sins, save us from the fires of hell, lead all souls to heaven, especially those most in need of thy mercy.*

We pray and we hope, but we do not *know* that that will be the case. I have a terrible fear that it will not be the case. If all are not saved, if many or most are lost, I do not know—despite the many or most explanations that have been proposed—how to square that with biblical passages and the theo-logic that suggest universal redemption. But God knows, and that is enough. We know that we are to proclaim the saving gospel. We know what we hope will be the case, but we know these things in the full recognition that the ultimate working out of God's mercy and justice eludes our certain grasp.[24]

Avery Cardinal Dulles

Avery Cardinal Dulles was well known in the United States. Although his article deals more explicitly with the understanding of hell, and whether or how many may be there, he cannot avoid the related opinions about universalism. After citing the traditional scriptural references—some for and some against universalism— then the church fathers —some for (Origen, Gregory of Nyssa, etc.) and some against (Augustine, Aquinas, Bellarmine, etc.)—and some church documents, he then discusses briefly Balthasar's views and those of Neuhaus. Then he gives his summary:

> It is unfair and incorrect to accuse either Balthasar or Neuhaus of teaching that no one goes to hell. They grant that it is probable that some or even many do go there, but they assert, on the ground that God is capable of bringing any sinner to repentance, that we have a

24. Neuhaus, *Will All Be Saved?*

right to hope and pray that all will be saved. The fact that something is highly improbable need not prevent us from hoping and praying that it will happen. According to the Catechism of the Catholic Church, "In hope, the church prays for all men to be saved" (1 Tim 2:4) (CCC #1821). At another point the Catechism declares: "The church prays that no one should be lost" (CCC #1058).

One might ask at this point whether there has been any shift in Catholic theology on the matter. The answer appears to be yes, although the shift is not as dramatic as some imagine. The earlier pessimism was based on the unwarranted assumption that explicit Christian faith is absolutely necessary for salvation. This assumption has been corrected, particularly at Vatican II. There has also been a healthy reaction against the type of preaching that revels in depicting the sufferings of the damned in the most lurid possible light. An example would be the fictional sermon on hell that James Joyce recounts in his *Portrait of the Artist as a Young Man*. This kind of preaching fosters an image of God as an unloving and cruel tyrant, and in some cases leads to a complete denial of hell or even to atheism.

Today a kind of thoughtless optimism is the more prevalent error. Quite apart from what theologians teach, popular piety has become saccharine. Unable to grasp the rationale for eternal punishment, many Christians take it almost for granted that everyone, or practically everyone, must be saved. The Mass for the Dead has turned into a Mass of the Resurrection, which sometimes seems to celebrate not so much the resurrection of the Lord as the salvation of the deceased, without any reference to sin and punishment. More education is needed to convince people that they ought to fear God who, as Jesus taught, can punish soul and body together in hell (Matt 10:28).

The search for numbers in the demography of hell is futile. God in His wisdom has seen fit not to disclose any statistics. Several sayings of Jesus in the gospels give the impression that the majority are lost. Paul, without denying the likelihood that some sinners will die without sufficient repentance, teaches that the grace of Christ is more powerful than sin: "Where sin increased, grace abounded all the more" (Rom 5:20). Passages such as these permit us to hope that very many, if not all, will be saved.

All told, it is good that God has left us without exact information. If we knew that virtually everybody would be damned, we would be tempted to despair. If we knew that all, or nearly all, are saved, we might become presumptuous. If we knew that some fixed percent, say fifty, would be saved, we would be caught in an unholy rivalry. We would rejoice in every sign that others were among the lost, since our own chances of election would thereby be increased. Such a competitive spirit would hardly be compatible with the gospel.

We are forbidden to seek our own salvation in a selfish and egotistical way. We are keepers of our brothers and sisters. The more we work for their salvation, the more of God's favor we can expect for ourselves. Those of us who believe and make use of the means that God has provided for the forgiveness of sins and the reform of life have no reason to fear. We can be sure that Christ, who died on the Cross for us, will not fail to give us the grace we need. We know that in all things God works for the good of those who love Him, and that if we persevere in that love, nothing whatever can separate us from Christ (cf. Romans 8:28–39). That is all the assurance we can have, and it should be enough.[25]

25. Dulles, "The Population of Hell."

— 5 —

Twentieth-Century Orthodox Authors

Vladimir Soloviev (1853–1900)

ALTHOUGH SOLOVIEV BELONGS TO the nineteenth century I include him here. He is considered by many to be the greatest religious thinker in Russian history, so his thoughts on our topic are very important. He was the mentor of Florensky, Bulgakov, and many of the most prominent thinkers of the Russian Religious Renaissance. (This is the designation given to some of the best intellectuals and holy people who were expelled from the Soviet Union and birthed the greatest Russian thought and spirituality of their whole history. And it happened outside of their home country.)

As we shall see, the Russians—Soloviev, Florensky, Bulgakov, and Berdyaev—are very strong on the *corporate nature of salvation.* At the heart of Russian thinking about the gospel is the transfiguration of the *whole cosmos.* Quotes within this article by Gustafson are from Soloviev.

> Salvation inevitably takes its ancient Christian form of restoration. Soloviev marks his early adherence to this idea by his repeated reference in the original Greek to Origen's famous version of it: "the restoration of all things" *(apokatastasis ton panton).* What distinguishes Soloviev's doctrine of salvation from the patristic tradition of Eastern Christianity is his application of the idea of deification not to the individual monk contemplating in the monastery but to all human beings living in the world community. The ultimate task of salvation is not personal but universal; it is deified mankind. Deified mankind is thus equated with the idea of the Kingdom of

> God, and the attainment of it is a form of the Origenist restoration of all things.[1]

A friend of mine just received his doctorate with a dissertation on Soloviev. I asked him if he thought Soloviev was a universalist. He wrote:

> Solov'ev's idea of divine-humanity, first explicitly expressed in the final Lectures on Divine Humanity (1881), is the central and constant theme in his thought. Essentially divine-humanity is Solov'ev's re-appropriation and development of the patristic doctrine of deification, most fully expressed by St. Maximus the Confessor. Solov've significantly develops his teaching about divine-humanity in *Spiritual Foundations* where he emphasises the personal and ecclesial aspects of deification. He gives it is fullest expression in *Justification of the Good,* a work which integrates realist and moral approaches to deification. A number of questions naturally emerge from a study of Solov'ev's teaching about deification, in particular: To what extent was Solov'ev a universalist? Does the idea of divine-humanity or the deification of humanity imply the salvation of all? How does the idea of *apokatastasis* relate to deification? What answers does the patristic tradition give to these latter two questions? To what extent and in what ways has Solov'ev developed the patristic doctrine of deification? The following reflections are limited simply to consideration of the first question—was Solov've a universalist?
>
> Initial reflections on this question lead to an affirmation of Solov've as a universalist. His conception of deification as divine-humanity, as the whole of humanity divinized, would appear to demand it. In *Lectures 11 and 12* Solov'ev sets out the foundations of his teaching, namely, that through the Incarnation of Christ, humanity shares in the divine-human union. Solov'ev's presentation of deification is a theology of the gradual extension of the incarnation to take in the whole human race and indeed the whole natural order. Particular emphasis is placed on the corporate dimension of humanity and in terms of salvation this anthropology—patristic in origin—implies that no one is saved alone but rather communally. Additionally Solov'ev highlights the ontological implications of the Incarnation for humanity, namely, that after the birth of Christ, humankind exists in or can come to share in a new, divine-human order of being. All this logically implies that

1. Gustafson, "Soloviev's Doctrine of Salvation," 31–47.

> Solov'ev's early teaching about divine-humanity naturally supports the idea of universal salvation.[2]

Pavel Florensky. *The Pillar and Ground of Truth*

This is one of the most profound books I have ever read. Florensky is considered one of the great Russian minds of our times. He was a polymath who was allowed to teach in his clerical garb in the University of Moscow during the Communist era because of his expertise in many sciences. He died in the gulag. His teaching concerning universalism (although he didn't use that word) is extremely important as he had a comprehensive vision of the whole of the Eastern and Western traditions. Thus his views on universalism are not derived from any one particular historical period or particular theology. His views will be important as an introduction to Sergius Bulgakov whose mentor he was. The quotes are all from his "Letter Eight, Gehenna," in *The Pillar.*

> But who does not know that nearly every soul is now infected with a more or less vulgar Origenism, with the secret belief that one will ultimately be "forgiven" by God? So often do people of various estates and positions make this admission that one begins to think that there is some sort of internal inevitability here. Indeed, there *is* inevitability here. Consciousness proceeds from the idea of God as Love. Love cannot create in order to ruin; it cannot create, knowing of death; Love cannot fail to forgive. The idea of retribution directed toward creation and all that is creaturely is dispersed in the light of immeasurable Divine Love as a mist is dispersed by the rays of the all-triumphant sun. From the point of view of eternity, everything is forgiven, everything is forgotten: "God will be all in all" (1 Cor 15:28). In brief, the impossibility of universal salvation is impossible.
>
> That is how it is from the height of the idea of God. But, taking the bi-conjugate point of view, i.e., proceeding not from God's love of creation but from creation's love of God, the same consciousness inevitably arrives at the diametrically opposite conclusion. Now consciousness cannot admit that there could be salvation without the answering love of God. And since it is also impossible to admit that love is unfree, that God has compelled creation to

2. Jeremy Pilch, author of *Breathing the Spirit*, email correspondence with author, January 15, 2015.

love, it inevitably follows that it is possible that God's love could exist without creation answering His love. In other words, the impossibility of universal salvation is possible.

"For none can lay a foundation other than the one that is there, namely Jesus Christ. If anyone builds on this foundation with gold, silver, precious stones, wood, hay, or straw, the work of each will come to light, for the Day will disclose it. It will be revealed with fire, and the fire [itself] will test the quality of each one's work. If the work stands that someone built upon the foundation, that person will receive a wage. But if someone's work is burned up, that one will suffer loss; the person will be saved, but only as through fire" (1 Cor 3: 11–15).

In the next verse (1 Cor 3:16) the Apostle hurries to explain why "he himself shall be saved." Because you, believers, he writes to the Corinthians, "are temples of God" and the "temple of God is holy," and the Spirit of God dwells in this temple. What is holy cannot perish, disappear, or abide in fire. What is given by Christ to man *as man* cannot perish. Otherwise the image of God would perish. But this image must abide. The holy abides; man's holy essence is saved. But its "work" can perish for this essence. The entire content of consciousness will perish to the extent that it is not from faith, hope, and love. "He himself (autos) shall be saved."

A man with evil will can in no wise be forced to change this will. But as long as he does not change it, he will not be reformed. Sin cannot be removed from a man without touching his inner essence. But on the other hand, we cannot imagine a man who is absolutely and thoroughly corrupt, for this would mean that God's creation has not succeeded. The image of God cannot perish. Only one conclusion is possible from this, a conclusion which was drawn by us before, i.e., antimony.

Thus, if you ask me, "will there in fact be eternal torments?" I would answer "Yes." But if you were also to ask me, "Will there be universal restoration in bliss?" I would again say "yes." The two are thesis and antithesis. I think that only the view expounded here satisfies both the spirit and the letter of the Holy Scripture as well as the spirit of patristic writing. But, being inwardly antinomic, this view requires faith and absolutely does not fit into the plane of rationality. It is neither a simple "yes" nor a simple "no." It is both "yes" and "no." It is an antinomy. This indeed is the best proof of its religious validity.[3]

3. Florensky, *The Pillar and the Ground of Truth*, 153–86.

"Antinomic" and "antimony" may need a word of clarification. Robert Slesinski is one of the authorities on Florensky. He writes:

> But, then, just what does he understand by the term, antimony? Florensky uses the term in the sense of the *apparent* contradiction between demonstrated propositions. For him, an antimony is an opposition whose terms remain incompatible in the *logical* order, but which find their resolution and, indeed, essential complementarity solely in the metalogical order. The opposition is such that it cannot be disentangled by discursive reasoning, nor is it accessible to intellectual intuition.[4]

Trevor Hart

Trevor Hart, an Evangelical, speaks here generally of our knowledge of God, but his comment would apply to our knowledge of God's will concerning eschatological realities. He expresses this same antimony of Florensky in this way:

> Perhaps the fact that we cannot capture that meaning and pin it down in neat logical formulae bothers us. But is this anything more than our *eschatological impatience*, which always seems to want certainty and clarity now, rather than resting content in the assumption that what we are granted now is sufficient, and being happy to wait for that time when we shall know fully, even as we are known.[5]

Sergius Bulgakov

Bulgakov is considered by many to be the greatest Russian theologian of the twentieth century. He was expelled from the Soviet Union and lived the rest of his life in Paris at the St. Sergius Institute. I give some of Gavrilyuk's basic teachings of Bulgakov concerning our topic; I will not go into the few difficulties he has with some of Bulgakov's views.

> Bulgakov recognized that numerous biblical passages spoke of the punishment of hell as *aiwvios*. He argued that the popular conception of eternity as an infinite duration of time was flawed. For one

4. Slesinski, *Pavel Florensky*, 145.
5. Hart, *Nothing Greater, Nothing Better*, 113.

thing, such infinite duration would have a beginning at the point of human death. More importantly, on a forensic model, an infinite application of punishment for temporal sins is unjustly cruel. Even according to human standards, such punishment would be far greater than the crime. Thus, observed Bulgakov, the idea of infinite retributive punishment led to an anthropomorphic and unbecoming image of a vengeful and cruel deity.

Bulgakov claims that to admit the eternal perdition of a single rational creature is to limit the wisdom and goodness of God. Creaturely freedom, no matter how obstinate and persistent in evil, cannot become a permanent barrier to the power of God's grace. The moral unity of humankind and the ontological sharing in one corporeality do not allow the eternal separation of all into the two separate categories of the saved and of the permanently damned.

Bulgakov envisioned the eventual restoration of Satan and the fallen angels along with all human beings. Bulgakov claimed that the complete repentance and conversion of all angelic beings, including Satan, was inevitable.

Bulgakov's universalism moved beyond a faithful commentary on patristic material. His development of the insights of Gregory of Nyssa and Isaac of Nineveh is in many ways daring and original. The recognition of the limitless character of God's love moves one to embrace universalism, whereas the recognition of creaturely freedom to permanently reject God leads to the admission of eternal hell. Bulgakov's eschatological shift from juridical to ontological categories may be termed "ontological universalism."

Bulgakov's ontological universalism may also be distinguished from so-called hopeful universalism, which found its influential twentieth century advocates in Hans Urs Von Balthasar and Karl Rahner. The Russian theologian saw the universal purgation that resulted in the universal restoration of all things to God neither as a paradox nor as a hope, but as an ontological necessity—ontological universalism.

It is undeniable that Bulgakov's universalism, especially his shift from juridical to ontological categories, from what he called "penal code theory" to the eschatology of participation in the life of God, opens a fresh dimension that has not yet been sufficiently explored in the Western accounts of eschatology.[6]

6. Gavrilyuk, "The Ontological Universalism of Sergius Bulgakov," 292–302 .

Staretz Silouan

Silouan was one of the great modern Russian staretzes from Mt. Athos. Kallistos Ware quotes from Sophrony's *Life of Silouan*:

> It was particularly characteristic of Staretz Silouan to pray for the dead suffering in the hell of separation from God. He could not bear to think that anyone would languish in "outer darkness." I remember a conversation between him and a certain hermit, who declared with evident satisfaction, "God will punish all atheists. They will burn in everlasting fire."
>
> Obviously upset, the Staretz said, "Tell me, supposing you went to paradise, and there looked down and saw somebody burning in hell-fire—would you feel happy?"
>
> "It can't be helped. It would be their own fault," said the hermit.
>
> The Staretz answered him with a sorrowful countenance. "Love could not bear that," he said. "We must pray for all."[7]

Nicholai Berdyaev

One of the unique contributions I found in Deak's study was his treatment of the Orthodox philosopher Nicholai Berdyaev (1874–1948). He is considered one of the outstanding Christian philosophers of the twentieth century. He also was one of the intellectuals who became an outstanding member of the Russian Religious Renaissance. His views, therefore, relevant to our topic, are very significant and important. Except for a few minor nuances, I found that Berdyaev agrees with most of the positions presented in this *Guide*. Quotes within are from Berdyaev.

> "The idea of an eternal hell is absurd and evil." Berdyaev deplores the idea that there is a link between the idea of hell and the notion of justice. [He] warns that "the weakness of eschatological thought lies in its tendency to return into time, when the matter in question concerns eternity." Especially concerning the doctrine of hell, an unobjectifiable event becomes objectified. "I pray every day for those who suffer the torments of hell; and in so doing I assume that these torments are not eternal." "There is no justice in punishing by *eternal* torments sins committed in time."

7. Ware, *The Inner Kingdom*, 194.

"The greatest religious and moral truth to which man must grow is that *we cannot be saved individually.* My salvation presupposes the salvation of others also, the salvation of my neighbor; it presupposes universal salvation, the salvation of the whole world, the transfiguration of the world." It may be puzzling for some that Berdyaev, who is one of the principal advocates of universal salvation in our century, in his writings more than once rejects the solution of the problem of *apokatastasis* offered by Origen. [Deak explains the reason for this disagreement, but shows how Berdyaev's solution also leads to universalism.] As early as in the 1920s and early 1930s we find the idea of universal salvation clearly developed from the principle of solidarity of mankind. God not only *wants* all to be saved, but He will *in reality* effect this through the free-co-operation of man, so that when time runs out and gives place to eternity, He will indeed.[8]

Kallistos Ware

Kallistos Ware is a very significant modern witness to universalism. Although he himself concludes with a *hope* for the salvation of all, throughout his study he refers to Christians who go further and believe that everyone will be saved. One of these—besides the frequently cited fathers such as Origen and Gregory of Nyssa—is Isaac the Syrian. I turn to Ware for a treatment of this great father of the Syrian Church who believed in *apokatastasis.* Quotes within are from St. Isaac.

> A third patristic author who dared to hope for the salvation of all was St. Isaac of Nineveh, honored and loved throughout the Christian East as "Isaac the Syrian." Particularly striking is Isaac's understanding of hell. He insists that the texts in the New Testament about fire, the worm, outer darkness, and the gnashing of teeth are not to be understood literally and in a physical sense. Isaac had a better answer. In his view the real torment in hell consists, not in burning by material fire, nor in any physical pain, but in the pangs of conscience that a person suffers on realizing that he or she has rejected the love of God:
>
> "Also I say that even those who are scourged in hell are tormented with the scourgings of love.
>
> "The scourges that result from love—that is, the scourges of those who have become aware that they have sinned against

8. Deak, *Apocatastasis,* 20–40.

love—are harder and more bitter than the torments which result from fear.

"The pain that gnaws the heart as the result of sinning against love is sharper than all other torments that there are.

"It is wrong to imagine that the sinners in hell are deprived of the love of God. But the power of love works in two ways: it torments those who have sinned, just as happens among friends here on earth; but to those who have observed its duties, love gives delight."

When I first came across this passage as a student more than forty years ago, I said to myself: That is the only view of hell that makes any sense to me.

Now if all this is true—if, as Isaac says, those in hell are not cut off from the love of God, and if, as C.S. Lewis asserts, they are self-imprisoned—then may it not be that they still have some hope of redemption? (Indeed, the Orthodox Church says a special prayer for them at Vespers on the Sunday of Pentecost.) If divine love is constantly knocking on the door of their heart, and if that door is locked on the inside, may not the time come when at long last they respond to love's invitation and open the door! If the reason for their suffering is that they recognize how grievously they have sinned against love, does this not imply that there is still within them some spark of goodness, some possibility of repentance and restoration?

Isaac, for his part, definitely believed that this was so. In the second part of his Homilies he speaks of a "wonderful outcome" that God will bring to pass at the end of history:

> "I am of the opinion that He is going to manifest some wonderful outcome, a matter of immense and ineffable compassion on the part of the glorious Creator, with respect to the ordering of this difficult matter of Gehenna's torment: out of it the wealth of His love and power and wisdom will become known all the more—and so will the insistent might of the waves of His goodness.
>
> It is not the way of the compassionate Maker to create rational beings in order to deliver them over mercilessly to unending affliction."

Isaac is convinced that 'not even the immense wickedness of the demons can overcome the measure of God's goodness, quoting Diodore of Tarsus. Unquenchable and limitless as it is, God's love will eventually triumph over evil: "There exists with Him a single love and compassion which is spread out over all creation, a love which is without alteration, timeless and everlasting. No part belonging to any single one of all rational beings will be lost." Here, then, in distant Mesopotamia, is one who is not afraid to affirm with Julian of Norwich and T.S. Eliot, "all shall be well, and all manner of thing shall be well."

Our belief in human freedom means that we have no right to categorically affirm "All must be saved." But our faith in God's love makes us dare to hope that all will be saved.[9]

Olivier Clement

Clement is a convert to Russian Orthodoxy and fairly well known for his work *The Roots of Christian Mysticism.* But in that book he hardly touches at all upon our theme of *apokatastasis.* However, in his book *On Being Human: A Spiritual Anthropology*, there is a section worth quoting. He mentions, briefly, a number of viewpoints we have seen in my present study. He would certainly agree that we should *hope* for the salvation of all.

> All the complexity of our nature, shaped as it has been by the dramatic events of history, and by the ways we have used and misused our freedom; all the ambiguity, henceforth transfigured, of the "garments of skins" will find a place in the Kingdom; in the being that was created wholly good we have used our freedom to dig holes of nothingness; but we shall discover to our amazement that they have become the wounds in Christ's hands and feet, through which the divine life comes to us and will come to us forever.
>
> First we should notice that the early church, all expectant for Christ's return, scarcely acknowledged the existence of any who had been damned for all eternity, any more than it acknowledged that the saints would enjoy an immediate consummation and bliss. The Fathers were more often concerned with the notion of purification and progressive healing.
>
> For some of the dead, locked in ignorance or hostility, the early church knew that peace, or silence, or the glimpse of the divine Doctor would be experienced as torments; but prayer was offered wholeheartedly for all the dead, especially for those making this journey through the underworld, those, in other words, who are in hell.
>
> In all the Eastern rites, at vespers for Pentecost, there are ancient "kneeling prayers." The Byzantine version reads: "In this feast

9. Ware, *The Inner Kingdom*, 206–15.

of fullness and salvation, thou dost graciously hear our prayers of atonement for those who are shut in hell and givest us the great hope of seeing thee grant to the departed the deliverance from the evils which condemn them." The love of God, multiplied by the prayer of the church, works from within—for no one is alone—upon the ultimate hell, individual solitude, to open it to the communion of the Kingdom that is coming.

Thus it was that the undivided church rejected universal salvation as a doctrine, but adopted it as something to hope and pray for. The last word of Christianity is not hell but victory over hell; God does not promise us universal salvation because he can only offer it to us and wait for our response, our love, to let it happen.[10]

10. Clement, *On Being Human*, 149–52.

— 6 —

Twentieth-Century Protestant Theologians

Before we go into specific theologians I will give a list of the talks given at a conference, "Universalism and the Problem of Hell." It is not important that you know who the speakers were. This is a *Guide* to stimulate your interest for your own future research. I want to make the point in this treatment of the twentieth century that the subject of universalism is not some obscure and suspect topic that needs to be hushed up and not spoken about too publicly and freely for fear of scandalizing people! It has been the subject of major—mostly Protestant—conferences, and there is a vast amount of literature available. At the time of this writing, I am not aware that any major Catholic conference has been dedicated to this theme. The chapter headings indicate the talks that were given:

- Universalism: Two Distinct Types. Trevor Hart
- Universal Salvation in Origen and Maximus. Frederick W. Norris
- *Descensus* and Universalism: Some Historical Patterns of Interpretation. Daniel A. du Toit
- The Nineteenth- and Twentieth-Century Debates about Hell and Universalism. David J. Powys
- The Case for Conditional Immortality. John W. Wenham
- The Case Against Conditionalism: A Response to Edward William Fudge. Kendall S. Harmon

- The Atonement: The Singularity of Christ and the Finality of the Cross: The Atonement and the Moral Order. Thomas Torrance
- Are They Few That Be Saved? Paul Helm
- Everlasting Punishment and the Problem of Evil. Henri Blocher.

Karl Barth

Karl Barth is considered by many to be the greatest protestant theologian of the twentieth century. Was he a dogmatic universalist, believing that the salvation of all men and women is both necessary and guaranteed? Some think yes, that the logic of his theology leads to this, although he never took the step himself. Others say that this latter opinion is a misunderstanding of his theology. I will briefly present an argument on each side, from articles by Colwell and Greggs.

John Colwell on Barth

> Perhaps it is necessary to clarify from the beginning that while Barth consistently rejects universalism as a doctrine, he certainly does not reject the possibility that all men and women may ultimately be saved. If it is presumptuous for those who advocate universalism to suggest that God is in some way obliged to save all men and women, then it is equally presumptuous to suggest that he is obliged *not* to do so. But to admit the possibility of the ultimate salvation of all men and women, to hope for it and even to pray for it falls well short of the opinion that the salvation of all men and women is both necessary and guaranteed.[1]

Colwell's attempt to clarify Barth's position is quite complicated and profound. It's not necessary to go into it here. The heart of it concerns the relationship between God's freedom and the freedom of the human person. Colwell's key is an analysis of the nature of God's time in this relationship. It is neither "timelessness" nor "eternity" but "pure simultaneity." This means that the salvation of each individual has not been determined by some "timeless" decision by God from all eternity, but is a result of a contemporaneous relation between God and each person. Quoting Barth: "In Jesus Christ it comes about that God takes time to Himself, that He Himself, the

1. Colwell, "The Contemporaneity of the Divine Decision," 140–41.

eternal One, becomes temporal, that He is present for us in the form of our own existence and our own world, not simply embracing our time and ruling it, but submitting Himself to it, and permitting created time to become and be the form of His eternity."

Barth is against any abstract theory that would limit God's freedom. In his understanding of the contemporaneity of the human and divine he allows for the possibility of disobedience. In reference to this freedom Colwell has this amazing statement: "For Barth, the possibility of reprobation is not excluded by the constancy of God's love for men and women but is itself a manifestation of that love, the love in which God allows human disobedience to be real albeit in the form of an impossible possibility."[2]

Tom Greggs

Tom Greggs is one of the major theologians on the question, "Was Barth a universalist?" His summary that I present here is representative of those who consider Barth a universalist *in a certain sense.*

> Although Barth rejects *apokatastasis,* all are saved in Christ's election of humanity. Whether or not this amounts to universalism is a hugely disputed area. Although the logic of Barth's theology clearly seems to point in a Universalist direction, Barth himself at various points in his theology emphatically denied that he was a Universalist.
>
> In this much, it may seem that Barth simply presents a dialectic which cannot be resolved, and demands instead recognition of the mystery of the work of God. However, it is difficult to deny that Barth's theology tends very strongly in a Universalist direction. Towards the end of Barth's career he wrote regarding universalism:
>
>> It would be well not to yield to that panic fright which this word [universalism] seems to have a way of spreading around it, at least before one has come to an understanding with regard to its possible sense or nonsense.
>>
>> It would be well, in view of the "danger" with which the expression is ever and again seen to be encompassed, to ask for a moment, whether on the whole the "danger" from those theologians who are forever sceptically critical, who are again and again suspiciously questioning, because they are always fundamentally legalistic, and who

2. Ibid., 150, 144.

> are therefore in essentials sullen and dismal, is not in the meantime always more threatening amongst us than that of an unsuitably cheerful indifferentism or even antinomianism, to which one would in fact yield oneself on one definite understanding of that conception.
>
> One thing is sure, that there is no theological justification for setting any limits on our side to the friendliness of God towards man which appeared in Jesus Christ.
>
> Furthermore, this emphasis on the particularity of salvation in Jesus Christ ensures that the sovereignty of God is in no way depreciated by the universal salvation, but chooses to bind himself to creation in the particular person of Jesus Christ. That Barth rejects dogmatic universalism on occasion does not mean that Barth posits a limitation on the friendliness of Jesus Christ. Rather, Barth's rejection of universalism posits a limitation of the problems that can arise from such a universal scope for salvation—namely, lack of particularity. Barth, therefore, rejects universalism *as a principle* but he advocates the total and final victory of Christ *as a person*: his universalism is one which entirely arises from particularity. *Barth is a new type of universalist, whose universalism recognizes that there can be no undermining of particularity*." (my emphasis)[3]

The purpose of Greggs's book is not simply to quote Origen's and Barth's views side by side, but to engage them in a creative dialogue. After presenting their positions on certain aspects of the faith, he then has a section for each called "Symphony," where he tries to present his attempt at their dialogue. What follows are selections of his "Symphony" about "Universalism in Christ."

> In both Origen and Barth, one is able to see a particularist approach to universalism, grounded in the second person of the Trinity's particular (or appropriate) universal work. This universal work is in the being of the Son: the person and work of Christ cannot be separated. It is objective participation in the second person (as *logika* in the Logos or as humans in Christ's humanity) which all humanity shares, whether one responds to it or not, and it is this that determines that both the theologies of Origen and Barth point in a universalist direction.
>
> This universalism is grounded in a firm sense of the will and power of God to save all humanity. Indeed, so strong in each theologian is the sense of God's desire and ability to save all humanity

3. Greggs, *Barth, Origen, and Universal Salvation*, 29–41.

that they even offer hope for Judas Iscariot. Judas becomes the archetype of universal salvation: if salvation can include even him, it can include all humanity; if salvation is the will of God, it cannot be avoided even in the present rejection of God's salvation.

All humanity is united in Jesus Christ and the plan and will of God. Origen and Barth's universalism recognizes that Christ's humanity (or reason) has implications for all humans regardless, in the first instance, of their varied responses to Him. This means that both theologians can have an ultimately positive view of the negative wretchedness of humanity in the graciousness of God's salvation.[4]

Balthasar on Barth

Balthasar's brief comment is relevant here: "Barth is led into the center of his theological concerns through this identity of divine justice and divine mercy; but then only a small turn is needed (Christ damned for all, so that all the damned arrive at salvation) in order to bring him dangerously near to the *apokatastasis panton, where I do not wish to follow him*" (my emphasis).[5]

As we have seen, Balthasar stopped at *hoping* all would be saved. He clearly states here that he understood Barth to go beyond his own position, and he did not wish to go there.

Jurgen Moltmann (1926–)

Jurgen Moltmann is considered one of the outstanding Protestant theologians of modern times.

Nicholas Ansell

I give here, according to Ansell, a very brief summary of Moltmann's eschatological views. Moltmann's centering his universalism on Christ's descent into Hell is *very traditional* as we shall see (below) in the theological and liturgical statements on this Christian mystery.

4. Ibid., 90–91
5. Balthasar, *Dare We Hope?*, 154.

[In Moltmann] we are presented with a view of universal salvation in which final Judgment is central to Christian hope. Here is a vision for the salvation of all people in which true human freedom is affirmed. Here is a universalism in which the cry of Justice is not to be silenced. Moltmann's eschatology, rooted in the theology of the cross, holds out the promise that in the end justice and mercy will embrace. After surveying a number of universalist and non-universalist arguments, both biblical and theological, Moltmann sets out his own position on the outcome of the Final Judgment entitled "Christ's Descent into Hell and the Restoration of All things." [Quotes with in the text are from Moltmann]

It is precisely here that the divine reason for the reconciliation of the universe is to be found. It is not the optimistic dream of a purified humanity, it is Christ's descent into hell that is the ground for the confidence that nothing be lost but that everything will be brought back again and gathered into the eternal kingdom of God. *The true Christian foundation for the hope of universal salvation is the theology of the cross, and the realistic consequence of the theology of the cross can only be the restoration of all things.*

The connection between this "existential" Hell and salvation for all is developed by the following three-fold claim:

"*Christ's descent into hell* therefore means: even in the experience of hell you are there (Ps 139:8)

"*Christ's descent into hell* means: you have suffered the experience of hell for us, so as to be beside us in our experience of hell.

"*Christ's descent into hell* means, finally, hell and death have been gathered up and ended in God."

Moltmann's train of thought in the three assertions should be interpreted as follows:

1. Because Christ descended into Hell, he (and thus God) is there in the Hell we experience today (a point made with an allusion to the language of Ps 139:8).
2. Through suffering Hell for us (or God in Christ) is beside us in our hells.
3. Through Christ's death and resurrection, God entered the "God-forsaken space" of Hell *for the first time*, thus taking it up into his omnipotence and overcoming its deadly power.

"In his forsakenness by the Father [Christ] experiences hell, because in pure obedience he seeks the Father *where he is not to be found*, and through his descent into hell takes hell and all those who are in it into his trinitarian fellowship with the Father."

Moltmann quotes Origen's legendary saying that Christ hangs on the cross as long as there is a sinner in hell. "God will in the end be all in all, *not because God's love overcomes the very last believer*, but because the shadows of Christ's cross dissolve hell."

Moltmann refers sympathetically to a line of thought developed by Urs von Balthasar that sought to mediate "in the spirit of Origen between the Eastern Fathers' concern for the assurance of salvation and Western theology's 'emotional emphasis on freedom."

"The theology of the Cross," writes Moltmann, "is the true Christian universalism. There is no distinction here, and there cannot be any more distinctions. All are sinners without distinction, and all will be made righteous without any merit on their part by his grace which has come to pass in Christ Jesus."[6]

Peter Phan

Balthasar's most distinctive and controversial contribution to eschatology is his theology of holy Saturday. Following the visionary experiences of Adrienne Von Speyer, he suggests that in addition to the crucifixion on holy Friday, there is also the mystery of Holy Saturday in which the crucified "descended into hell as a final act of self-kenosis and, in solidarity with the dead and the damned, took on the total self-estrangement from the Father. The Crucified`s descent into hell in solidarity with sinners, von Balthasar argues, *is the theological basis for the possibility of and the necessity of hope for apokatastasis.*" [my emphasis] [7]

Jürgen Moltmann writes:

The logic of hell is nothing other than the logic of human free will, in so far as this is identical with freedom of choice. The theological argument runs as follows: "God, whose being is love, preserves our human freedom, for freedom is the condition of love. Although God's love goes, and has gone, to the uttermost, plumbing the depth of hell, the possibility remains for each human being of a final rejection of God, and so of eternal life." Let us gather some arguments against this logic of hell.

The first conclusion, it seems to me, is that it is inhumane, for there are not many people who can enjoy free will where their

6. Ansell, *The Annihilation of Hell*, 36–39.

7. Phan, "Roman Catholic Theology," 225.

eternal fate in heaven or hell is concerned. Anyone who faces men and women with the choice of heaven or hell, does not merely expect too much of them. It leaves them in a state of uncertainty, because we cannot base the assurance of our salvation on the shaky ground of our own decision. Is the presupposition of this logic of hell perhaps an illusion—the presupposition that it all depends on the human beings' free will?

The logic of hell seems to me not merely inhumane but also extremely atheistic: here the human being in his freedom of choice is his own lord and god. His own will is his heaven—or his hell. God is merely the accessory who puts that will into effect. If I decide for heaven, God must put me there; if I decide for hell, he has to leave me there. If God has to abide by our free decision, then we can do with him what we like. Is that "the love of God?" Free human beings forge their own happiness and are their own executioners. They do not just dispose over their lives here; they decide on their eternal destinies as well. So they have no need of any God at all. After God has perhaps created us free as we are, he leaves us to our fate. Carried to this ultimate conclusion, the logic of hell is secular humanism, as Feuerbach, Marx and Nietzsche already perceived a long time ago.

The Christian doctrine of hell is to be found in the gospel of Christ's descent into hell. In the crucified Christ we see what hell is, because through him it has been overcome. Judgment is not God's last word. Judgment established in the world the divine righteousness on which the new creation is to be built. But God's last word is "Behold I make *all things* new" (Rev 21:5). From this no one is excluded. Love is God's compassion with the lost. Transforming grace is God's punishment for sinners. It is not the right to choose that defines the reality of human freedom. It is the doing of the good.[8]

Ansell gives us another quote from Moltmann:

It is only if a qualitative difference is made between God and human beings that God's decision and human decision can be valued and respected. God's decision "for us," and our decisions for faith or disbelief no more belong on the same level than do eternity and time. We should be measuring God and the human being by the same yardstick if we were to ask: what, and how much, does God

8. Moltmann, "The Logic of Hell," 43–47.

do for the salvation of human beings, and what, and how much, must human beings do?[9]

J. M. Shaw

The theologian J. M. Shaw, writing from his position at Queen's Theological College in Kingston, Ontario, in 1945, is unique for his time as he gives a very balanced theological view of the question of *apokatastasis*. He finally opts for annihilationism; his balanced position concerning this choice is worth quoting:

> The Universalist view, however, while thus recognizing in its most persuasive representatives the eternal penalty involved in sin, does not, we think, sufficiently regard or recognize the fact of the possibility of final refusal as involved in the very nature of moral personality. To affirm dogmatically Universal Restoration or Salvation is in our judgment to ignore or at least to minimize unduly the fact that in the very nature of the case, God's patient and pursuing love notwithstanding, the destiny of a moral and spiritual personality is in the last issue committed to itself and depends upon its personal self-willed choice.
>
> So we must confess that in our judgment at least as between the two alternative views of Universalism and Conditional or Potential Immortality, the latter, with its recognition of the possibility of ultimate extinction or annihilation for any who are finally impenitent, is the more consistent at once with the totality of Scripture teaching and with the moral probabilities of the case.
>
> But on this matter we do well not to be dogmatic. For those in Christ at death the future is one of unspeakable glory and blessedness. "Eye hath not seen nor ear heard, neither have entered into the heart of man the things which God hath prepared for them that love Him" (1 Cor. 2:9). For those on the other hand who continue to reject the proffer of God's love in Christ here and hereafter, if any such there be, the future is one of darkness and defeat, equally beyond our power to conceive. So much at least is certain, and this is sufficient for our guidance in the present.[10]

9. Ansell, *The Annihilation of Hell*, 381.
10. Shaw, *Life after Death*, 104–5.

Paul S. Fiddes

Fiddes is a University Research Lecturer in Theology in Oxford and a significant Christian writer and scholar. He is conversant with most of the literature used in the present *Guide*. There is a section of his book where he presents what he calls "dogmatic universalism" and "hopeful universalism." This distinction corresponds to Deak's understanding of *apokatastasis* and universalism: the first believes in the *inevitability* of salvation for all; the second believes in the *possibility* of salvation for all. I present here Fiddes's understanding of hopeful universalism as it is the one he opts for.

> The second kind of universalism is a hopeful one. It believes that it is *possible* for all created persons from the beginning of time to enter into the communion of God's triune life, and it hopes that this will indeed happen. This hope has secure foundation in the power of God's love to draw all persons into response; and since this love is embodied eternally in the cross and resurrection of Jesus all salvation is inseparable from these Gospel events. But this view still leaves open the terrible possibility that some created persons may go on insisting on separation from God for eternity, preferring the satisfaction of being enclosed in themselves rather than opening themselves to the challenge and healing of divine love.
>
> Some image of eternity close to the second option has the advantage of taking seriously the freedom God has granted to creation. It also allows to God the humility of being willing to be rejected; it adds another dimension to the tragedy within the victory of love in considering God's eternal vision of potentials that have not been actualized. The point of a "hopeful universalism" is to take seriously both the questing love of God and the need for the free co-operation of responsible creatures, and so there needs to be scope for these factors to be worked out and for hope to be fully realized.
>
> There must be a realistic context where it is *possible* for God's desire "that all human beings should find salvation and come to know the truth" (1 Tim 2:4) to be fulfilled, and the space between the bounds of birth and death does not seem sufficient. There must be some limitless opportunities for God to offer love in the divine quest for reconciliation, and for created beings to respond.
>
> A dogmatic universalism tends towards a view of instantaneous transformation of the most wicked villain through the moment of judgement, painful though it will be to face the truth. It fits with a view of eternity as the simultaneity of time, where no future development is possible or needed. A hopeful universalism

leaves scope for a longer process of self-understanding, repentance and growth into perfection and this requires a model of eternal life where there is some kind of time and becoming. In my view, this is the most coherent picture of human destiny available, if we are to hope for eternal life at all, and take a wager on the power of love in the universe.[11]

Biblical Rationales for Universal Salvation

Harmon

A common objection to the universalism of the Alexandrian school—Clement, Origen, and Gregory of Nyssa—is that it was more rooted in Platonism or Neoplatonism or even in Gnosticism than in Scripture. This is not true. Neither Plato nor Plotinus nor the Gnostics taught universalism. Harmon gives an exhaustive presentation of how the three great universalists of this Alexandrian school used scripture in their treatment of *apokatastasis*. He offers a fairly comprehensive survey of the scriptural texts used by these fathers. Here is the conclusion of his study.

> Although all three authors are now remembered as allegorical exegetes, their direct appeals to biblical texts as support for their eschatological universalism were rooted in a very literal reading of these texts. Their exegesis became more allegorical when they dealt with passages which, when read literally, seemed to contravene the understanding of eschatological punishment they were advocating. Origen frequently reinterpreted such texts as references to psychological torment rather than physical torment and freely redefined the meaning of "eternal" with reference to punishment.
>
> It was Gregory, however, who developed the allegorical approach to these texts more fully, and finding in the *theoria* of these passages a different nature and purpose of punishment than which the 'letter' of the texts expressed.
>
> Clement, Origen, and Gregory were each influenced by Greek philosophy as well as by the sacred Scriptures in the development of their understanding of apokatastasis. However, whatever the other sources for the development of their concepts of universal salvation may have been, it is certain that they believed their ideas to be firmly rooted in the Scriptures. Evaluation of whether they

11. Fiddes, *The Promised End*, 194–96.

were right in this reading of the biblical texts is more appropriately the task of a study in biblical or systematic theology.[12]

Matt 25:31–36. The Sheep and the Goats

This is the gospel passage most used by those refuting universalism, and it is the one that universalists have had to come to grips with the most. From Harmon I give the approach of Gregory of Nyssa.

> Matt 25:31–46. References to all or part of Matt. 25:31–46 occur thirty times in Gregory's corpus. Eighteen of these references are to v. 31 alone or focus on portions of the passage that refer only to the reward of the righteous and therefore have little relevance for the issue at hand. Nine additional references mention the division of humanity into the "sheep" and the "goats" and/or the respective reward or retribution for each group; but elaboration that might clarify Gregory's understanding of this text and its relationship to his views on eschatological punishment is absent or insignificant in these passages.
>
> The remaining four references are supplied with more suggestive commentary; three of them emphasize the retributive aspect of eschatological punishment. In *De beneficentia* Gregory referred to vv. 31–46 and described the judgment of evil, misanthropic persons as "fiery eternal punishment." Two passages from the *Orationes de beatitudinibus* in which Gregory employed phrases from vv. 31–34, 40, 41, and 45 highlight the division between the two groups of people and portray the punishment meted out to the wicked as retribution; but Gregory offered no clarification of the duration either of the division of the faithful from the wicked or of the punishment of the wicked.
>
> An allusion to v. 41 in P*asch* however, suggests the possibility of an end to the torment of the "goats": because the "just punishment of fire" is imposed only on the body and does not harm the soul, the soul will be raised. The predominant emphasis on retribution in Gregory's use of this passage is attributable to Gregory's homiletic agenda: the majority of the references appear in the course of discussions of the reward of the faithful and biblical texts that warn of the judgment of the wicked underscore the consequences of the hearer's or reader's decisions and deeds. Gregory's

12. Harmon, *Every Knee Should Bow*, 128–29.

rhetorical purposes thus minimize any ostensive influence of his concept of *apokatastasis* upon his exegesis of this text.[13]

Jersak

One of the interminable areas concerning the whole question of universalism is the interpretation of Scripture: Is it for or against universalism? Jersak presents an exhaustive study of hell and Gehenna in the Scriptures to arrive at an answer to this question. As you will see, his answer is *neither*:

> The stubborn fact is that Scripture is richly polyphonic on the topic of hell and judgment—*as if by design.* Thus, if we become dogmatic about any one position, we reduce ourselves to reading selectively or doing interpretive violence to those verses that don't fit our chosen view. Our theological prejudices blind us to passages we may have read many times but never really seen. Even a tentative removal of traditional lenses leads to the question, "Why didn't I ever see that verse before?"
>
> The complexity of the text is not a deficiency! If we can momentarily suspend our penchant for forcing the text to harmonize with our systems or even with itself, we'll see some magnificent tensions between those old Moroccan leather covers.
>
> For example, the bible repeatedly affirms that God has given humanity the real capacity for authentic choice. To choose between life and death, heaven and hell, and the mercy and wrath implies the real possibility that some could choose the way that leads to destruction. The bible testifies that some may opt for choices that result in permanent posthumous exclusion (the lake of fire, outer darkness, etc.)
>
> On the other hand, the Bible just as plainly teaches that God is also free: free to relent, free to forgive, free to restore even when judgment is promised, free to pursue lost sheep "until he finds them," free to play out a cosmic history where, in the end, "every knee will bow," "all things will be restored," "everything will reconciled," and "all will be made alive," a time when absolutely everything will be "summed up in Christ," and when Christ will, in turn, hand a saved cosmos over to his Father so "that God may be all in all." The Alpha purposes of God for the universe will come to their Omega point in Jesus Christ. Thus, before we plant our flag

13. Ibid., 106.

on any one version of hell, we must take all of the biblical texts on hell and judgment, mercy and restoration into account.

These three types of passages, which I will call infernalist, annihilationist, and universalist texts, cannot be integrated easily into a cogent dogmatic system. In fact, my argument for hope over presumption is just this: the Bible doesn't allow us to settle easily on any of these as "isms." Perhaps that's because humankind needs all of these voices. Maybe God would have the wicked tremble before the infernalist passages and renounce their evil ways. He would comfort the afflicted with the promise of justice and a day of accounting, and he would have "the elect" embrace the broader hope of the Universalist verses. We joyfully hope for the best but bow heart and knee to the justice and mercy of God. Thus, one voice cannot be absolutized without negating the others. Our obsessive attempts to harmonize the Scriptures into artificially coherent, stackable propositions—as if they required us to contend for their reliability or authority—actually do violence to their richness.

So where does that leave us? Rather than painting themselves into Universalist or infernalist corners, a great many of the church Fathers and early Christians found refuge in the humility of hope. They maintained the *possibility* (not the presumption) of some version of judgment and hell and the presumption that at the end of the day, no one need suffer it forever. For several centuries, scholars and mystics engaged in experimental theology, warning that none should presume upon universal redemption because of the possibility of damnation, *and* that none should presume upon hell for anyone else other than perhaps oneself. For them, peace came not from certainty of knowing how it would all turn out but from a solid hope in God's great love and mercy—that Jesus' plan to save the whole world might actually work.

This book will address the central problem of this "heated" debate: *not* infernalism versus annihilation versus universalism, but rather, authentic, biblical Christian hope vis-à-vis the error of dogmatic presumption (of any view). The data summarized herein did lead me to four conclusions, which you may or may not share after all is said and done:

1. We cannot presume to know that all will be saved or that anyone will not be saved.
2. The revelation of God in Christ includes real warnings about the possibility of damnation for some *and also* the real possibility that redemption may extend to all.

3. We not only dare and hope and pray that God's mercy would finally triumph over judgment; the love of God *obligates* us to such hope.
4. Revelation 21–22 provides a test case for a biblical theology of eschatological hope. Rev 21:25: On no day will its gates ever be shut, for there will be no night there.

Even a superficial reading of the Gospels reveals one point very clearly: Jesus steadfastly refused to address in a systematic way abstract theological questions, especially those concerning the age to come. His whole manner of expressing himself, the incessant use of hyperbole and riddle, of parable and colorful stories, was intended to awaken the spiritual imagination of his disciples and to leave room for reinterpretation as they matured in the faith; *it was not intended to provide final answers to their theological questions.* [my italics]

Jesus never intended for anyone to take the details of a parable literally; the details merely provided a colorful background for the main point, which itself is not always easy to discern. So as a first step towards understanding the parable of the sheep and the goats, we must try to discover its main point.

Is the main point really a moral about the eternal destiny of the good and the bad? I doubt it. As I read the parable anyway, its main point is truly startling. When we feed the hungry and provide drink to the thirsty, says Jesus, it is as if we are offering food and drink for Jesus himself; and when we refuse to do this, it is again as if we are refusing to offer it to Jesus himself. In order to make this point in a forceful way, Jesus tells a colorful story in which those who are judged are utterly surprised to discover the true nature of their own actions.

As is true of all parables, furthermore, we could easily draw all kinds of faulty inferences if we should take the details of this one too literally. We might conclude that eternal life is simply a reward for our own good works—something that Paul, at least, explicitly denies; or we might conclude that, whether we repent or not, any of us who have ever failed to meet our responsibilities to others—which is to say all of us—are destined for eternal punishment. Such inference, however, would take us far beyond the main point of the story.[14]

14. Jersak, *Her Gates Will Never be Shut*, 6–10, 84–85.

Balthasar on Matt 25: 31–46

Everywhere in the writings of the synoptic evangelists, the main concern is the requirement for sympathetic understanding and for emulation of absolute and unrelenting love as Jesus himself exemplifies this in his love of God and of his neighbor; indeed, as he conclusively formulates it in a central, twofold command (Mt 22:37–40). As I said, the closing portrayal by Matthew (25:31–46) is at heart nothing but the definitively valid requirement behind this command; and indeed, in the sense that love for Christ the "King" (v.34) is measured by love as shown in practice for our fellowmen, who stand in need of help and love in many and varied respects (vv. 40,45).

Even if this scene is described in line with the Old Testament images of trial and on the basis of the unrelentingness of the New Testament either-or, as a judgment with a twofold outcome, it is [quoting Rahner] *not to be read as an anticipatory report* about something that will someday come into being but rather as a disclosure of the situation in which the person addressed now *truly* exists. He is the subject who is placed in the position of having to make a decision with irrevocable consequences; he is the one who, by rejecting God's offer of salvation, can become lost once and for all.

Regarding Mt 25, it should be added that Jesus is speaking to Jews who know no other form of divine judgment than one with a two-sided outcome, which means that the framework of the parable is not new; but, above all, the picture that it frames: the basis of judgment, New Testament morality means that doing or not doing to one's neighbor is acting or not acting with respect to Christ himself.[15]

Parry and Partridge, *Universal Salvation?*

These editors are among the foremost advocates of Christian universalism. I simply give the authors and titles of the chapters—with a brief quotation—to motivate your interest and to keep showing you the variety and extent of the modern discussion about universalism. It is one of the books I highly recommend you read.

15. Balthasar, *Dare We Hope?*, 31–32.

I single out Thomas Talbott because he is close to the top of the list of modern evangelical universalists. (We have seen his interpretation of the sheep and the goats parable.) He has the first three chapters in the book, and the other authors were asked to agree or disagree with his views. This shows his stature as a universalist, that he is the center of this discussion as presented by the editors.

Talbott—Towards a Better Understanding of Universalism

Talbott—Christ Victorious

Talbott—A Pauline Interpretation of Divine Judgement

Like many of my conservative evangelical friends, I tend to view the entire Bible through a Pauline lens. But unlike most conservative evangelicals, I see no way to escape the conclusion that St. Paul was an obvious Universalist.

Howard Marshall—The New Testament Does *Not* Teach Universal Salvation.

The New Testament does not teach nor imply universal salvation. It teaches that some will be lost. That is why there is such an urgency to proclaim the gospel to all the world.

Thomas Johnson—A Wideness in God's Mercy: Universalism in the Bible.

The case for universalism is stronger than is usually realized. Eventually, everyone will confess Jesus Christ as Lord. The traditional view that the vast majority of people who have ever lived will suffer in a hell of eternal conscious torment is inconsistent with the biblical data.

Jerry Walls—A Philosophical Critique of Talbott's Universalism

1. Since God's eternal nature is perfect love, he sincerely extends his grace to all his human creatures and does everything he can to elicit from them a free response of trust and love.
2. Although free creatures can decline God's love, his ultimate purpose of glorifying himself cannot be defeated since his love is demonstrated whether it is accepted or rejected.
3. Some sinners will never accept God's love and will be forever separated from him.

Eric Reitan—Human Freedom and the Impossibility of Eternal Damnation.

> It is not enough to turn down God once. It must be done *forever.* But in order for anyone to be eternally damned . . . the person must unwaveringly choose to reject God at every moment for the rest of eternity, *even though the person sees absolutely no good reason for doing so, has every reason not to do so, and has absolutely no compelling desire to do so.* Is *that* really possible? It certainly seems hard to imagine anyone making such a choice.
>
> **Daniel Strange**—A Calvinist Response to Talbott's Universalism
> However, far from believing the existence of hell was a cause of distress for the redeemed Calvinist of the stature of Johnathan Edwards and Murray McCheyne wrote that believers will rejoice in the existence of hell. The basis for their argument is not a feeling of superiority or a perverse sadism but can be summed up by McCheyne himself: "The redeemed will have no mind but God's. They will have no joy but what the Lord has." From the perspective of heaven we will rejoice in all of God's perfections including his just judgement of those who have rebelled against him.
>
> **John Sanders**—A Freewill Theist's Response to Talbott's Universalism
> I remain unpersuaded that universalism is true. My main criticisms are: 1) it seems Talbott . . . is committed to some form of an eschatological lobotomy on the redeemed; 2) his understanding of divine risk-taking is too limited; 3) his criteria for "free and rational" choices means that neither Adam nor ourselves have ever been free or rational; 4) that these criteria imply that God has to make us godlike in order for us to choose God; 5) that he seems to understand sin in a mechanical sort of way that is readily overcome by proper education; 6) that God seems morally culpable for bringing evil in the world; and 7) that his use of a soul-making theodicy puts him further away from Arminianisn than perhaps he believes he has gone.[16]

Jan Bonda

One of the driving motivations for seeking to find justification for belief in universalism is to obliterate the terrifying image of God that eternal punishment has implanted in the minds and hearts of the people of the world. We have come up with all kinds of sophisticated rationalizations to

16. Parry and Partridge, *Universal Salvation?*, 48, 74, 97, 123, 136, 164, 185–86.

put these two concepts together: a God of love and eternal punishment. Bonda's book is one of the best I have come across which reinterprets biblical statements with the eyes of a universalist. All I can do is give a taste of how he has done this, especially in Pauline texts.

One of the themes which points to universalism is the liturgy of the church. It is often remarked that the faith was expressed in the liturgy before the written biblical texts. And, it is well known that the letters of Paul contain some liturgical hymns. Keeping this in mind, the first of Bonda's commentaries I will present is on the great hymn of Phil 2:8–11:

"And being found in human form, he humbled himself and became obedient to the point of death—even death on a cross. Therefore God also highly exalted him and gave him the name that is above every name, so that at the name of Jesus every knee should bend, in heaven and on earth and under the earth, and every tongue should confess that Jesus Christ is Lord to the glory of God the Father."

> Regarding [this text] it has been said that Paul has only believers in mind. The supporters of this view will have to prove that Paul does not refer to salvation for all the world. In this instance surely it cannot be maintained that it only applies to believers. For when Paul says that every tongue will praise God, there is no alternative: this includes everyone. For the apostle here deals with the judgment seat of God. And no one will want to deny that all people, believers as well as unbelievers, will have to appear before his judgment seat. So, all who appear before the judgment seat will also bend their knees before God to praise him.[17]

As mentioned above, the gospel passage about the Last Judgment (Matt 25:31–46) is often referenced as the most convincing biblical proof of eternal punishment, and consequently refuting the possibility of the salvation of all. Here is Bonda`s explanation. Of course, many will disagree, but it is another example of how, in this book, with Universalist eyes, he gives an interpretation different from the traditional one.

> We are told that there is forgiveness for all sin and blasphemy except blasphemy against the Spirit (Matt 12:31). Let us limit ourselves to the sins Jesus lists in Matt 25:31–46. Verse 46, in particular, has always been cited as undeniable proof that Jesus taught eternal punishment. Yet it is clear that the sins Jesus lists in this passage do not constitute the blasphemy against the Spirit.

17. Bonda, *The One Purpose of God*, 221.

Assuming that Jesus did not utter this severe word with the intention of contradicting what he said moments before we must accept that the sins mentioned in this passage will eventually be forgiven. *This means, however strange this may sound to us, that this statement of Jesus about eternal punishment is not the final word for those who are condemned.*"(Italics in text)

This text (Matt 25:46) in particular plays a major role in the doctrine of eternal punishment. Jesus does not follow it up with a word of salvation after punishment, to put us at ease. But something else does follow. Here is the word in its immediate context (26:1-2):

"And these will go away into eternal punishment, but the righteous into eternal life. When Jesus had finished saying all these things, he said to his disciples: 'You know that after two days the Passover is coming and the Son of Man will be handed over to be crucified.'"

People have become accustomed to reading Jesus' words about eternal punishment and eternal life as a description of the dual finale of history. And that is what they are. They not only constitute a serious warning, but they also describe what actually happens in the judgment. Did Jesus see this as the *end* of all things? Did he say: "That is how it will end; this is how God wanted it"—and did he simply acquiesce in it? That is precisely what he did not do, as we are told in the subsequent verses. Jesus does not shift the focus to something that differs from what he has been discussing. He seems to be totally taken aback by the terrible nature of this finale.

But then he speaks about what he must do. He now approaches his death. Now his life will be given as a ransom for many (literally, in exchange for many (Matt 20:28). His blood will be poured out for many. Twice we read: "for many." Who are these "many"? They are the many who have entered the wide gate and walk the easy road that leads to destruction (Matt 7:13; cf. Matt 22:14). These are the same people of whom he just said that they will end in "eternal punishment."

But did he not give his life for "the few" who found the narrow road that leads to life (Matt 7:14)? Certainly, also for them. But when he speaks of these "many," he does not refer to these "few"! He is the Lamb of God who takes away "the sins of the world" (John 1:29), "and he is the atoning sacrifice for our sins, and not for ours only but also for the sins of the whole world" (John 2:2).

One who thinks that in Matt 25:46 Jesus announces the end of the history of the world as an outcome we simply have to accept, acts as if the entire history of Jesus' suffering and death does not affect the many who go to eternal punishment. Jesus goes the way of the cross in order to open for these many the way of escape from eternal punishment; to make sure that their "going away to eternal punishment" will be followed by their return.

We have from the beginning of this book wrestling with a single question: What is God like? Since Augustine, our tradition has taught us that God has two separate goals. He has predestined a small percentage of humankind to salvation, to eternal life. The rest of humanity has been predestined to eternal damnation. Since it is his will that many will be lost, we have no option but to acquiesce.

Our starting point was the question: Is it God's will that we passively accept the perdition of our fellow human beings? There can be no denial: the bible teaches us that this is not his will. Being called by God means being called not to acquiesce in the perdition of our fellow human beings. This we discovered in the story of Abraham and his intercession for Sodom, in the story of Moses and his intercession for Israel, and in Jesus' parable of the prodigal son. We noticed this, in particular, in Jesus' ministry. He heals every sickness and disease, and when he sees crowds, he is moved with compassion for them. He regards them as sheep without a shepherd, as harvest that is at risk of being lost. And the calling of his disciples is to be workers in that harvest.[18]

John Hick.

Hick's book is often quoted in discussions about evil and the God who is love. I recommend it as a good presentation of this theological question. He surveys a number of authors in the history of Christianity. I present here his over-all conclusion relevant to our topic of universalism.

> Indeed misery which is eternal and therefore infinite would constitute the largest part of the problem of evil. For the doctrine of hell has as its implied premise either that God does not desire to save all His human creatures, in which case He is only limitedly good, or that His purpose has finally failed in the case of some—and indeed, according to the theological tradition, most—of them, in which case He is only limitedly sovereign. I therefore believe that the needs of Christian theodicy compel us to repudiate the idea of eternal punishment.

18. Ibid., 70, 217–18, 256.

Does this mean that we are led to universalism, in the sense of a belief in the ultimate salvation of all human souls? [No] There remains the third possibility of either the divine annihilation or the dwindling out of existence of the finally lost. This is a very dubious doctrine of Christian theism to sponsor, and not one in which we should acquiesce except for want of any viable alternative. But in fact an alternative is available: namely, that God will eventually succeed in His purpose of winning all men to Himself in faith and love. The question, then, is whether God *can* eventually do for the free creatures that He has created what He *wants* to do for them.

The difficulty that is more often felt about the idea of universal salvation concerns God's power to evoke a right response in personal beings that He has endowed with the fateful gift of freedom. Can God *cause* them to respond to Him without thereby turning them into puppets? The least that we must say, surely, is that God will never cease to desire and actively to work for the salvation of each created person. He will never abandon any as irredeemably evil. However long an individual may reject his Maker, salvation will remain an open possibility to which God is ever trying to draw him.

Can we go beyond this and affirm that somehow, sooner or later, God will succeed in His loving purpose? It seems to me that we can, and that the needs of theodicy compel us to do so. God has made us for Himself, and our whole being seeks its fulfillment in relation to Him. He can influence us both through the world without and by the activity of His Holy Spirit within us, though always in ways that preserve the integrity and freedom of the human spirit. It seems morally (although still not logically) impossible that the infinite resourcefulness of infinite love working in unlimited time should be eternally frustrated, and the creature reject its own good, presented to it in an endless range of ways. We cannot say in advance *how* God will eventually free all created souls from their bondage to sin and establish them in love and glad obedience towards Himself, but despite the logical possibility of failure, the probability of His success amounts, as it seems to me, to a practical certainty.[19]

19. Hick, *Evil and the God of Love*, 277–80.

Twentieth-Century Protestant Theologians

Gregory MacDonald (Robin Parry)

If you are thinking of perhaps buying another book to continue your reading, I would suggest this one. MacDonald's Introduction to this edited work is entitled "Between Heresy and Dogma," and is one of the best short treatments of the question, "Is Universalism Heretical?"[20]

20. MacDonald, *All Shall Be Well*, 1–25.

— 7 —

Notable Modern Universalists

George MacDonald. (1824–1905)

I WILL PRESUME THAT the reader knows something of who George MacDonald was—an inspiration to Tolkien, C. S. Lewis, and Chesterton, to name only a few of the most outstanding benefactors of MacDonald's deep insights into the human condition and Christianity.

Michael Phillips is one of the foremost scholars on MacDonald. After forty years of study he wrote: "It has been the single highest goal of my professional life to correctly and accurately understand George MacDonald's perspectives and then represent them favorably to our generation."

He poses the question:

> Did MacDonald believe in universal reconciliation? (To my knowledge the words "universalism" or "universal reconciliation" never once appear in MacDonald's writings.) Though I am reluctant to do so for the sake of stumbling those whose personal journeys of faith have not yet grown accustomed to the spiritual mountain air of these high regions of scriptural inquiry, for the sake of those who have been reading MacDonald for years, I am compelled to answer *yes.* My reading of Macdonald is that ultimately (no matter how many eons of purifying fire it takes), all created souls *will* ultimately (under the operation of infinite love and divine compulsion) avail themselves of the ceaseless wooing of Infinite Love.
>
> I find MacDonald's conclusion to the sermon "The Consuming Fire" as offering an intriguing window into his own heart

concerning God's potential ultimate redemption of all men. After quoting [from Revelations] *and hell itself will pass away*, MacDonald writes, "For then our poor brothers and sisters, every one shall have been burnt clean and brought home." This would seem to state it plainly and definitely.

Yet, in the middle of the sentence, an intensely personal aside, MacDonald cries out in prayerful plea, revealing his "hope"—"*We trust you, God, to bring them home . . . surely you will bring them home . . . you must bring them home!*" Then he adds the words that arise so frequently in his writings, probing the very heart of God: "*Then indeed wilt thou be all in all. Shall a man be more merciful than God? Shall all his glories, his mercy alone not be infinite? Would he not die yet again to save one brother more?*"

MacDonald thus concludes: "*As for us, now we will come to thee, our Consuming fire. And thou wilt not burn us more than we can bear. But thou wilt burn us. And although thou seem to slay us, yet will we trust in thee.*"[1]

So, as (C.S.) Lewis also conceded: "it is objected that the ultimate loss of a single soul means the defeat of omnipotence. And so it does." But MacDonald found the very idea of such a defeat almost inconceivable: "Those who believe that God will thus be defeated by many souls, must surely be of those who do not believe he cares enough to do his very best for them. He *is* their father; he had the power to make them out of himself, separate from himself, and capable of being one with him; surely he will somehow save and keep them! Not the power of sin itself can close *all* the channels between creating and created."[2]

William Barclay

William Barclay may be the most well-known of all the authors I am quoting in this *Guide*. His "Daily Study Bible Series" is on many a bookshelf. His understanding of universalism is based on a lifetime of meditation on the Scriptures. He may not be considered to be at the top of present day biblical scholarship, but his reflection on universalism comes from a lifetime of

1. Phillips, "George MacDonald and the Larger Hope, Part 1," Father of Inklings, http://fatheroftheinklings.com/behind-the-wardrobe/topics-on-gods-justice-the-atonement-and-the-potentiality-of-universal-reconciliation/george-macdonald-and-universal-reconciliation-part-1/ (accessed June 13, 2015).

2. Talbott, "The Just Mercy of God," 240.

prayerful meditation on the whole of the Scriptures. You will notice that he cites passages and makes comments similar to others who hold this opinion. After briefly mentioning the views of Origen and Gregory of Nyssa, which we have seen, he writes:

> I am a convinced Universalist. I believe that in the end all men will be gathered into the love of God. I want to set down not the arguments of others but the thoughts which have persuaded me personally of universal salvation.
>
> First, there is the fact that there are things in the New Testament which more than justify this belief. Jesus said, "When I am lifted up from the earth I will draw *all* men to myself." Paul writes to the Romans: "God consigned *all* men to disobedience that he may have mercy on *all*." He writes to the Corinthians, "As in Adam *all* die, so in Christ shall *all* be saved."
>
> I believe that it is impossible to set limits to the grace of God. I believe that not only in this world, but in any other world there may be, the grace of God is still effective, still operative, still at work. I do not believe that the operation of the grace of God is limited to this world. I believe that the grace of God is as wide as the universe.
>
> I believe implicitly in the ultimate and complete triumph of God, the time when all things will be subject to him, and when God will be everything to everyone (1 Cor 15:24–28). For me this has certain consequences. If one man remains outside the love of God at the end of time, it means that that one man has defeated the love of God—and that is impossible. Further, there is only one way in which we can think of the triumph of God. If God was no more than a King or Judge, then it would be possible to speak of his triumph, if his enemies were agonizing in hell or were totally and completely obliterated and wiped out.
>
> But God is not only King and Judge; God is *Father*—he is indeed Father more than anything else. No father could be happy while there were members of his family for ever in agony. No father would count it a triumph to obliterate the disobedient members of his family. The only triumph a father can know is to have all his family back home. The only victory love can enjoy is the day when its offer of love is answered by the return of love. The only possible final triumph is a universe loved by and in love with God.[3]

3. Barclay, *A Spiritual Autobiography* , 65–67.

Jacques Ellul.

Jacques Ellul was one of the most perceptive Christian voices of the twentieth century. He is one of my mentors. He was a Calvinist and therefore generally of the Augustinian tradition.

Balthasar on Calvinism

> The position of Calvin and of classical Calvinism is too familiar to require detailed description: the twofold division of mankind into the chosen and the damned is so unequivocal that we can tell empirically, from the character of their unbelief or weak belief, that they belong to the latter class. In *Institutio*, III , 2, Calvin describes the "pure and clear knowledge" that our belief in the redemptive work of Christ through the Holy Spirit has engendered in our hearts and lists the identifying signs that distinguish this authentic belief from the "infirm and transitory" one of the damned. They "never attain this secret inner revelation of their salvation, which Scripture ascribes only to the chosen."
>
> Thus, for Calvin's successors, "the certainty of salvation and of the state of grace" is "the essential characteristic of belief and the most immediate effect that faith produces in the consciousness of the chosen . . . and immediate *certitude absoluta*, occurring together with belief itself."[4]

Considering Ellul's Calvinist background, I was all the more surprised to read his opinions about universalism. They come from one of his last books. His teaching was always firmly based on Scripture. It is one of the most succinct and clearest explanations of universalism that I know.

> I am taking up here a basic theme. It is the recognition that all people from the beginning of time are saved by God in Jesus Christ, that they have all been recipients of his grace no matter what they have done. This is a scandalous proposition. It shocks our spontaneous sense of justice. How can Hitler and Stalin be among the saved? The just ought to be recognized as such and the wicked condemned. But in my view this is purely human logic which simply shows that there is no understanding of salvation by grace or of the meaning of the death of Jesus Christ.

4. Balthasar, *Dare We Hope?*, 195–96.

But I want to stress that I am speaking about *belief* in universal salvation. This is for me a matter of faith. I am not making a dogma or a principle of it. I can say only what I believe, not pretending to teach it doctrinally as the truth.

How can we conceive of him who is love ceasing to love one of his creatures? It is astounding that Christian theology should not have seen at a glance how impossible this idea is. Being love, God cannot send to hell the creation which he so loved that he gave his only Son for it. There is indeed a predestination but it can only be the one predestination to salvation. We are not free to decide and choose to be damned. To say that God presents us with the good news of the gospel and then leaves the final issue to our free choice either to accept it and be saved or to reject it and be lost is foolish. In this case it is we who finally decide our own salvation.

It is certain that being saved or lost does not depend on our own free decision. He came to seek those who in strict justice ought to have been condemned. A theology of grace implies universal salvation. What could grace mean if it were granted only to some sinners and not to others according to an arbitrary decree that is totally contrary to the nature of our God?

As far as I know, none [of the texts] in either the Old or New Testament speaks about damnation or the damned. Many texts that refer to condemnation . . . do not have damnation in view at all but condemnation on earth and in time. God does not reject forever. He "will not keep his anger forever" (Ps 103:9). On the other hand, his mercy endures forever (Ps 106:1). These two great theological proclamations rule out the idea of a God who damns, for that would mean that he keeps his anger forever.

There are no greater or lesser sinners in the presence of the holiness, perfection, and absolute justice of God. All are sinners, and all as such have been assumed and reconciled to God by Jesus Christ. From the very outset this reconciliation is for all (Muslims, Buddhists, Nazis, Communist, etc.) and it will apply to them whether they know it or not, whether they will it or not. God is reconciled to them even if they are not reconciled to God. I stress again that our human will or disposition can do nothing to change what has been accomplished. I do not teach universal salvation. I announce it.[5]

5. Ellul, *What I Believe*, 188–209.

G. K. Chesterton

What follows is an opinion of Edward Babinski on the question whether or not Chesterton was a universalist. Admittedly his references are minimal but further research may, I believe, bolster his argument.

> Did G.K. buy into the notion of salvation for all? He wrote in ORTHODOXY: "*To hope for all souls is imperative, and it is quite tenable that their salvation is inevitable.*" Though he adds that such a view "is not specially favorable to activity or progress. In Christian morals, in short, it is wicked to call a man 'damned': but it is strictly religious and philosophic to call him damnable."
>
> I think Chesterton wanted to "lessen the impact" of his "tenability of universalism" in the face of church dogmas on damnation. So he combined the view that it was "quite tenable that their salvation is inevitable" with a practical view of damnation as a motivator.
>
> What Chesterton didn't realize or fess up to was that the threat of damnation is primarily a motivator for a person to join a particular Christian denomination and accept a particular soteriology (salvation theology), rather than a universal motivator to do good.
>
> I think people are motivated in a more universal fashion to do good by virtue of the fact that joys shared are doubled, while sorrows shared are halved. We are beings who have the same physical and psychological needs, fears, and pleasures. Few people enjoy having physical or psychological pains inflicted on them in word or deed; while the vast majority enjoy similar physical and psychological pleasures. Fear of damnation as I said seems to create more sects and divisions, each of which insists in the full acceptance of their soteriological beliefs as the only way to avoid damnation.

G.K. wanted to see more people become Christians, probably witty exuberant Christians like himself, "Chestertonianity," I'd call it. G.K. felt that Christianity (as he understood it,) made more sense and was more practical than other beliefs. However part of his belief was that he found universal salvation "quite tenable."[6]

We have seen that George MacDonald was a universalist. He was a significant influence upon Chesterton, and his influence would be a factor in any further demonstration of Chesterton's universalism.

6. Babinski, "G. K. Chesterton's Universalism."

C. S. Lewis?

Lewis is still probably one of the most read Christian writers in the world, and many may wonder if he was a universalist or not. It would be wonderful if we could include him as some kind of universalist. Unfortunately we cannot. I include him in my *Guide* as an example of an outstanding contemporary Christian writer who was not able to see his way to universalism; he is also a powerful witness to the reality of hell. This is even more curious as his great mentor, George MacDonald, was a universalist. Here is part of Thomas Talbott's explanation of Lewis's position (I omit Talbott's references).

> Few thoughtful Christians today, it is true, accept the idea of an eternal torture chamber; and according to some, particularly those who follow the lead of C. S. Lewis, hell is a freely embraced condition rather than an externally imposed punishment. In Lewis' own words, "I willingly believe that the damned are, in one sense, successful, rebels to the end; that the doors of hell are locked on the *inside*." It is not God who rejects the sinner forever, in other words; it is the sinner who finally rejects God forever. Nor is it God who ultimately defeats the sinner; it is the sinner who ultimately defeats God. So, as Lewis also conceded: "It is objected that the ultimate loss of a single soul means he defeat of omnipotence. And so it does."
>
> But MacDonald found the very idea of such a defeat almost inconceivable: "Those who believe that God will thus be defeated by many souls must surely be of those who do not believe he cares enough to do his very best for them. He *is* their Father; he had the power to make them out of himself, separate from himself, and capable of being one with him; surely he will somehow save and keep them! Not the power of sin itself can close *all* the channels between creating and created."
>
> Here, I believe, is the one point in MacDonald that C.S. Lewis seems not to have appreciated sufficiently: there can be no ultimate triumph of God's justice or righteousness, according to MacDonald, apart from a triumph of his love, because both require the absolute destruction of sin. The failure to appreciate this point fully rendered Lewis' own defense of hell, as we encounter it in *The Problem of Pain,* fundamentally incoherent.
>
> MacDonald also understood the *nature* of hell very differently than Lewis did. For whereas Lewis depicted hell as a place where Satan rules (see *The Great Divorce)* and from which God is

utterly absent, MacDonald regarded both hell and the lake of fire as special manifestations of God's holy *presence*.

This difference also manifests itself in their respective understandings of the image of fire. According to Lewis, "The prevalent image of fire is significant because it combines the ideas of torment and destruction"; but, according to MacDonald, the importance of this image is that it combines the ideas of destruction and *purification*. As MacDonald never tired of reminding us, "our God is a consuming fire and the consuming fire of his love will in the end consume (or destroy) all that is false within us." So even the fires of hell exist for the purpose of the ultimate redemption of those in it. "Hell is God's and not the devil's. Hell is on the side of God and man, to free the child of God from the corruption of death."[7]

7. Talbott, "Just Mercy," 240–43.

— 8 —

Christ's Descent into Hell and Its Relevance for Universalism

THE QUESTIONS TO BE raised and treated in this section concern the relationship between the various theological reflections about the Descent into Hades and the theologumenon of universalism. Du Toit gives an excellent historical treatment of the *descensus* in the Christian tradition that forms a very good background to the later understanding of the *descensus.* Ongoing reflections concerning the *descensus* do not occur until the middle of the fourth century. (The doctrine is not in the Nicene Creed (325 AD), but it is in the Apostles Creed, "He descended into hell.") Some of Du Toit's research about the *descensus before* this time will be helpful.

Du Toit

> A study of the *descensus ad inferos* creates the impression that I can supply a foothold for the idea of universalism.
>
> The *descensus ad inferos* forms part of our traditional confession. Nevertheless it has always raised questions since medieval times and prompted attempts at new interpretations up till the present day. Perhaps more than any other article of faith it confronted the church with the question about the authority of the confession, in the wake of which all kinds of distinctions were introduced or re-employed, e.g., that between fundamental and

non-fundamental articles of faith, the acceptance of a hierarchy of truths, etc.[1]

According to Du Toit, the earliest Christian reflections about the *descensus* come from apocryphal sources:

> For the early Christians there was no clear demarcation between canonical and apocryphal sources. The earliest Christian writings of, for instance, Ignatius and Polycarp contain very few references to the descensus. It is clear that the descensus stories were well-known—only short and casual references, without the need of further explanation, are to be found in these writings. The main conclusion must be that the descensus at this time represents no critical issue with regard to faith or doctrine, and therefore receives no systematic treatment. The first motive connected with these references seems to be the concern for the Old Testament believers.
>
> The concern for the Old Testament believers is then connected to the more obvious matter, i.e., the motive of *preaching*. Jesus' ministry was characterized by his preaching and the proclamation of the gospel and it is only logical that this activity should be continued during his projected visit to the underworld. But it is certainly not for everyone. Nowhere whatsoever do we encounter the idea that the preaching to the deceased was aimed at all of them. The *descensus Christi* is a visit only to the good part where the faithful of the Old Testament waited.
>
> There is still no trace of any universalism. The central idea behind the *descensus* up till this stage of development was . . . the very sober stating of the fact that God had not forgotten the faithful of the Old Testament.
>
> In another sense, however, it was indeed utilized to demonstrate the *extent and comprehensiveness* of Christ's work of salvation—a "universalism" of quite another kind! To the early church his work was of such a radical nature that not only the living but also the dead in the underworld were affected; not only was it important for the life of heaven and on earth, but for the whole of cosmos, i.e. the underworld included.[2]

1. Du Toit, "Descensus and Universalism," 74.
2. Ibid., 79–80, 91.

The Doctrine of the Orthodox Church concerning "He Descended into Hell" (Apostles Creed)

The theology of who Christ freed when he descended into Hell is intimately connected with the question of universalism, even if, as mentioned above, it was not a factor in the earliest understanding of the *descensus.* It will be an ongoing theological question throughout the centuries of whether Christ led *everyone* out of hell after his resurrection, or only certain people—the just. If he led *everyone* out of hell, even the sinners, this will be a good argument that at the end of time he will also lead everyone into eternal life, even sinners. His preaching the gospel to all, and convincing all, is a foretaste of what he will do at the end of time. As we shall see, one of Alfeyev's conclusions is that what Christ did in his descent is a "prototype of the resurrection of the human soul—the mystical dimension of the teaching."

Archbishop Hilarion Alfeyev: *Christ, the Conqueror of Hell*

According to Alfeyev, it is a *doctrine* of the church, and the teaching of Scripture, that, after his death, Christ "went and preached to the spirits in prison" (1 Pet 3:18–19). The *interpretation of this mystery* of the faith is a *theologumenon.* Among the fathers and theologians, it is a question whether Christ delivered everyone in this prison or only those who accepted his preaching and those who were faithful to God (like the Old Testament figures depicted in the Orthodox icon of the Resurrection).

Since the scriptural evidence is minimal, I will give the author's brief summary, then, one famous interpretation from early Christian poetry (Miletus of Sardis). I will then concentrate briefly on the fathers in both the Orthodox and Catholic traditions after the early centuries.

In keeping with the main thrust of this present book I will be presenting mostly the texts that express that Christ freed *everyone* from this prison of death. I am endeavoring to show that universalism was *one* of the legitimate theologumena throughout Christian history, and especially in the early centuries. It was and is *one of the orthodox interpretations* as regards salvation. This view is frequently represented *in later centuries* in the theologizing about Christ's descent to the realm of the dead.

Scriptural Summary (Alfeyev):

Thus, already in the New Testament we encounter three themes which A. Grillmeier regards as fundamental to all early Christian literature: 1) Christ descending into hell and preaching to the souls of all those held there, not only to the righteous but also to the sinners *(theme of kerygma)*; 2) there is a certain relationship between Christ's descent into Hades and the sacrament of baptism *(baptismal theme)*; 3) Christ descending into Hades, vanquished hell and death *(theme of victory).*

Christian Poetry. Miletus of Sardis:

The Lord when he had clothed himself with man . . . arose from the dead and uttered this cry: "I am the one that destroyed death and triumphed over the enemy and trod down Hades and bound the strong one. I carried off man to the heights of heaven. I am the one, says the Christ. I come then, all you families of men who are compounded with sins, and receive forgiveness of sins, for I am your forgiveness." "[This text] shows that, already in second century hymnography, Christ's redemptive sacrifice was viewed as pertinent for all people without exception. Thus it speaks not of Christ saving the righteous but of his forgiving all 'those who sullied themselves with sin."

St. Ephrem the Syrian

Then Christ rose from the dead in the third hour of the day, and he took the saints with him to his Father; now all mankind shall receive salvation through the death of Christ. For one was judged instead of all men, and salvation and mercy came into the whole world. Moreover, one died in order that all might rise from the dead. And the Lord died on behalf of every one, in order that everyone should rise from the dead with Him. For having died, he put man on himself like a garment, and took him with him into the heavens, and man became one of one with him. He took him as a gift to his Father.

Gregory Nazianzen

He wrote a poem, *Christus Patiens,* in which one of the stanzas reads: "You descended into Hades and, having seized many arms [of the enemy] You became the overseer of those in the nether world. Having slain the custodians and the gatekeepers, He will return from there in order that everybody should recognize Him as Helper, Self-Rooted and Benefactor, who was slain by his own people out of jealousy."

It is clear from the passages quoted above that the author of *Christus Patiens* regards the descent into Hades as a redemptive feat, accomplished by Christ for the salvation of all humanity and not only for a particular group of people. By his descent Christ destroys Hades, illumines the human race and raises Adam, who personifies all of humanity.

Cyril of Alexandria

He showed the way to salvation not only to us, but also to the spirits in hell; having descended, he preached to those once disobedient, as Peter says. For it did not befit for love of man to be partial but the manifestation of this gift should have been extended to all nature. Having preached to the spirits in hell and having said "Go forth" to the prisoners, and "show yourselves" to those in prison on the third day, he resurrected his temple and again opened up to our nature the ascent to heaven, bringing himself to the Father as the beginning of humanity, pledging to those on earth the grace of communion in the Spirit.

Cyril clearly emphasises the universality of the salvation given by Christ to humanity. Perceiving the descent of Christ into Hades as salvific for the entire human race, he avoids limiting salvation to one part of humanity such as the Old Testament righteous.

Clearly Cyril perceives the victory of Christ over hell and death as complete and definitive. For him, hell loses authority both over those who are in its power and those who are to become its prey in the future. Thus the descent into Hades, a single and unique action, is perceived as a timeless event. The raised body of Christ becomes the guarantee of universal salvation, the beginning of the way leading human nature to ultimate deification.

We may sum up the teaching of the fourth-century Eastern fathers on the descent into Hades as follows: first, as a commonly accepted and indisputably integral part of the church's *kerygma*; second, as an event of universal significance with all the dead included in salvation; third, as an event of limited significance, with only particular categories of the dead included in salvation; fourth, as the accomplishment of the Savior's "economy," the crowning feat he performed in order to save all people; fifth, as the victory of Christ over the devil, hell, and death; and sixth, as the prototype of the resurrection of the human soul—the mystical dimension of the teaching.

Western Fathers

Hilary of Potiers

Writing in the fourth century, Hilarius repeatedly refers to the descent. He states, in particular, that by his death Christ "destroys the gates of brass, demolishes the bars of iron, redeems him whom he created after his image, and returns to him the sweetness of paradise." According to Hilarius, having descended into hell, Christ continued to be present in paradise.

At Christ's descent into Hades, death and corruption are obliterated: "He it is that slays death in hell, that strengthens the assurance of our hope by his resurrection, that destroys the corruption of human flesh by the glory of his body." Christ's victory over death has a universal character: "The Son of God is nailed to the cross; but on the cross God conquers human death. Christ, the Son of God, dies; but all flesh (*omnis caro)* is made alive in Christ. The Son of God is in hell; but man is carried back to heaven."

Jerome

We do not find in Jerome a clear answer to who was saved from hell by Christ's descent into it. In his "Interpretation of the Book of Jonah," Jerome claims that Christ descended into hell "in order to liberate *all* those who were locked there." However, in another passage from the same book, he speaks of Christ who "brought to life *many* people with Him."

Augustine

Augustine's teaching on the descent is rather contradictory. According to Augustine's views [of predestination] which are based on a literal interpretation of Romans 8:29–30, salvation will be granted by God to those who were predestined to it, while others will be damned. Thus the salvific effect of Christ's descent into Hades does not extend to those who were not predestined to salvation. Indeed, in one instance Augustine even explicitly refers to the "heresy" of those who claimed that, when Christ descended into hell, the unbelievers believed in him and were liberated.

> The Augustinian teaching on Christ's descent into Hades is expounded more fully in a letter addressed to Evodius. This letter, which contains a comprehensive interpretation of 1 Peter 3: 18–21, suggests that the teaching on the evacuation of all in hell and complete devastation of hell by the risen Christ, was widespread in his time. Augustine rejects its [1 Peter 3.18–21] traditional and commonly accepted understanding.[3]

Daley states: "Augustine's explanation of Jesus' *descensus ad inferos* after his death, mentioned in 1 Pet 3.19 is [thus]: he insists that Jesus visited not the just who were in the 'bosom of Abraham,' but sinners in the hell of the damned, and that he released at least some of them from their 'sorrows.' Apparently hell is not a permanent state for Augustine until the common passage of all creatures from time into eternity."[4]

Gregory the Great

"Responding to the question 'Who was liberated from hell by the risen Christ?' Gregory follows Augustine: he definitely rejects the opinion that Christ saved all those who believed in him and labels such opinion 'heresy.' Like Augustine, Gregory claims that only the 'elect' or the 'predestined' were freed."[5]

Western Doctrine after Gregory and St. Thomas Aquinas

In the Roman Church after Gregory the Great, belief in the partial victory of Christ over hell became commonly accepted, being confirmed by the Council of Toledo in AD 625. In the mid-seventh century Pope Boniface attacked the Irish missionary Clement for teaching that Christ released all those detained in hell, whether believers or non-believers.

The Latin doctrine on the descent of Christ into hell was systematized and brought to completion by the thirteenth-century theologian St. Thomas Aquinas. In his *Summa Theologiae* he divides hell into four "regions": first, purgatory, where sinners experience penal suffering; second, the hell of the

3. Alfeyev, *Christ the Conqueror of Hell*, 55, 20–89.
4. Daley, *The Hope of the Early Church*, 139.
5. Alfeyev, *Christ the Conqueror of Hell*, 94.

patriarchs, the abode of the Old Testament righteous before the coming of Christ; third, the hell of unbaptized children; and fourth, the hell of the damned. In response to the question "Into which hell did Christ descend?" Thomas Aquinas admits two possibilities: Christ descended either into all parts of hell or only in the parts where the righteous were imprisoned, whom he was to deliver.

The division of hell into four regions and the teaching on purgatory are alien to Eastern patristics. For the theologians, poets, and mystics of the Eastern Church, the descent of Christ into Hades remains, above all, a mystery praised in hymns and subject to various but indefinite assumptions.

The Teaching of the Catholic Church about Christ's Descent

Nicene Creed: There is no mention at all in the Nicene Creed of Christ's descent into hell.

The Apostles' Creed: ". . . was crucified, died and was buried; he descended into hell . . ."

Quicunque Vult, or the Creed of (Pseudo) St. Athanasius: ". . . Who suffered for our salvation, descended into hell, rose again the third day . . ."

The Catechism of the Catholic Church:

#633: "It is precisely these holy souls, who awaited their Savior in Abraham's bosom, whom Christ the Lord delivered when he descended into hell. Jesus did not descend into hell to deliver the damned, nor to destroy the hell of damnation, but to free the just who had gone before him."

#637 "In his human soul united to his divine person, the dead Christ went down to the realm of the dead. He opened heaven's gates for the just who had gone before him."[6]

As we shall see below, Balthasar has a different view about what Christ did in Hell. Whether or not Christ suffered in Hades, or exactly who he freed, are theologumena. We are interested in the second question.

Edward Oakes, SJ was one of the foremost Balthasar scholars. Concerning the above statements of the *Catechism*, he wrote:

> To be sure, this version of the Catechism was published after Balthasar died, and so he cannot be blamed for dissenting from that particular sentence, at least as formally taught. But that is

6. *Catechism of the Catholic Church.*

> not much of a defense, for the sentence was evidently formulated with him in mind. We know this because Christoph Cardinal Schonborn (Archbishop of Vienna and chairman of the drafting committee of the Catechism) said so: "This brief paragraph on Jesus' descent into hell keeps to what is the common property of the church's exegetical tradition. Newer interpretations, such as that of Hans Urs von Balthasar (on the contemplation of Holy Saturday), however profound and helpful they may be, have not yet experienced that reception which would justify their inclusion in the Catechism."[7]

Balthasar's reflections about Holy Saturday mostly concern whether Jesus suffered or not in Hades. This is not directly relevant to our discussion of *apokatastasis*. The phrase added to the *Catechism* concerns who was saved, all or some. Nonetheless, this phrase is still an opinion and not dogma, "*common property* of the church's exegetical tradition," as the Cardinal expressed it. It was not the common property of the first four centuries; and, as Bulgakov stated (above), there has never been a unified position on *apocatastasis.*

The Divine Office. The Liturgy of the Hours according to the Roman Rite

The Divine Office uses three readings on this topic, all of which clearly state that Christ freed *all* who were in hades.

The first is the ancient homily—author unknown—on the Descent on Holy Saturday, which clearly states that "the earth trembled and is still because God has fallen asleep in the flesh and he has raised up *all* who have slept ever since the world began" (my emphasis).[8]

The second reading occurs on the Friday of the Third Week of Easter by St. Ephrem, who believed that Christ freed everyone:

> Death had its own way when our Lord went out from Jerusalem carrying his cross; but when by a loud cry from that cross he summoned the dead from the underworld, death was powerless to prevent it. He who was also the carpenter's glorious son set up his cross above death's all-consuming jaws and led *the human race* into the dwelling place of life. Since a tree had brought about the

7. Oakes, "Von Balthasar. Hell and Heresy," 29.

8. *Divine Office*, Vol. II, 496.

downfall of mankind, it was upon a tree that *mankind* crossed over to the realm of life. We give glory to you who put on the body of a single mortal man and made it the source of life for *every other mortal man.* (my emphases)[9]

St. Maximus of Turin (Fifth Sunday of Easter)

Christ is risen! He has burst open the gates of hell and let the dead go free. The bodies of the blessed enter the holy city, and the dead are restored to the company of the living. There is an upward movement in the whole of creation, each element raising itself to something higher. We see hell restoring its victims to the upper regions, earth sending it buried dead to heaven, and heaven presenting the new arrivals to the Lord. In one and the same movement, our Savior's passion raises men from the depths, lifts them up from the earth, and sets them in the heights.[10]

The Orthodox Liturgy

The *octoechos* (The Book of the Eight Tones) contains liturgical texts for every day of the week beginning with Sunday. It could be argued that the very theme of Christ's descent into Hades is one of the main ideas of the *octoechos*, inseparably linked to the events of Christ's death and resurrection.

The hymnographers quite often identify themselves, and with them the entire church or even all mankind, with those who benefit from Christ's saving work. In their verses Christ's saving of the dead and the exodus from Hades were not "one-time" events that occurred in the past without significance for the present. These are events that transcend time, whose fruits were reaped not only by those who were imprisoned in hell before Christ's descent but also by future generations. This universal, transcendental significance of Christ's descent and victory over hell and death is stressed in the octoechos.

Finally, the texts of the octoechos very frequently (perhaps in thirty-five out of one hundred cases) speak of how Christ led *all* people out of hell:

9. Ibid., 735.

10. Ibid., 815, 156.

In a mortal body, O Life, you were acquainted with death . . . and having destroyed the corrupter, Supremely Exalted One, you raised *all* with you.

Your soul made divine, O Saviour, plundered the treasure of hell and raised with it the souls from every age; while your life-giving body became a source of incorruption for *all*.

You came down to my aid as far as hell, and having made a road to the resurrection for *all*, you went up once more.

The gate keepers of hell trembled when you were placed as a mortal in the sepulchre; for you destroyed the strength of death and gave incorruption to *all* the dead.

Numbered among the dead you bound the tyrant there, so delivering *all* from the bonds of hell by your Resurrection.

At your descent, O Christ, hell became a laughing stock and disgorged *all* with joy by your Resurrection.

Destroyed by death, the miserable one [death] lies without breath; for it, the strong one, could not endure the encounter with the divine life and is slain, and resurrection is granted to *all*.

If we add to the above texts those that speak of Christ's descent and victory as a complete "emptying" of hell, it becomes clear that the authors of the liturgical books saw Christ's descent as significant for *all people* without exception. Sometimes various categories of the dead are mentioned, such as "the pious" or "righteous," but nowhere do the hymns speak of selectivity—the existence of certain groups that were unaffected by Christ's descent.

Nowhere in the *octoechos* is it stated that Christ preached to the righteous but left sinners without his saving words, or that he led the holy fathers out of hell but left all the rest. It is never indicated that someone was excluded from God's providence for the salvation of people, accomplished in the death and resurrection of the Son of God.

Had Christ shed mercy only on the Old Testament righteous who awaited his coming, what miracle is this? Had he freed from Hades only the righteous, leaving behind the sinners, why would the "assembly of Angels" have been amazed? The descent into Hades does not fit in with our usual, human ideas of justice, retribution, fulfillment of duty, the rewarding of the righteous and the punishment of the guilty. Something extraordinary happened that made the angels shudder and be seized with wonder: Christ descended into Hades, destroyed its "strong holds" and "bars," unlocked the gates of hell, and "opened up the path of resurrection to all people." He opened up the way to paradise for everyone without exception.[11]

11. Alfeyev, *Christ the Conqueror of Hell*, 157–79.

9

The Significance of the *Descensus* for Modern Theologians

THE *DESCENSUS* IS BECOMING a focal point for theologians in working out their approach to universalism. We have seen the comments of Moltmann and his acknowledgment that his views are similar to those of Balthasar's. We turn now to the latter.

Salvation in the Abyss, Balthasar's *Mysterium Paschale*

> As Trintarian event the going to the dead is necessarily also an event of salvation. It is poor theology to limit this salvific happening in an a priori manner by affirming . . . that Christ was unable to bring any salvation to the "Hell properly so-called," *infernus damnatorum.* Following many of the Fathers, the great scholastic [Aquinas] set up just such *a prioristic* barriers. Once agreed that there were four subterranean "reception areas"—pre-Hell, Purgatory, the Hell of unbaptised infants and the true Hell of fire—theologians went on to ask just how far Christ had descended and to just what point his redemptive influence extended, whether by his personal presence, *presentia,* or merely by a simple effect, *effectus.*
>
> This whole construction must be laid to one side, since before Christ (and here the term "before" must be understood not in a chronological sense but in an ontological), there can be neither Hell nor Purgatory, but only that Hades (which at the most one

> might divide speculatively into an upper and a lower Hades, the inter-relationship of the two remaining obscure) whence Christ willed to deliver "us" by his solidarity with those who were (physically and spiritually) dead. But the desire to conclude from this that all human beings, before and after Christ, are henceforth saved, that Christ by his experience of Hell has emptied Hell, so that all fear of damnation is now without object, is a surrender to the opposite extreme.
>
> Despite all the exegetical objections that Origen's account may arouse, he was theologically correct: in "being with the dead", Christ brought the factor of mercy into what is imaged as the fire of the divine wrath: "Once Hades engulfed us all and held us firm. That is why Christ did not only come down to earth, but also under the earth . . . He found us all in the nether world . . . and brought us out from there not onto earth but into the Kingdom of heaven." Catholic dogma must, in any case, speak of a "universal purpose of redemption" (ever against the restrictions of a doctrine of double predestination).[1]

Lex orandi, lex credendi

As noted, one of Balthasar's arguments for hoping that everyone will be saved is that, in her prayers, the church expresses her faith—lex *orandi, lex credendi— and* the church prays for the salvation of all. Alfeyev's book is an examination of this *lex* as regards texts in the Orthodox liturgy that refer to Christ's descent into hell. I am mostly concerned with the question of *who* did Christ liberate in this descent?

> Loosely translated as "the law of praying is the law of believing" refers to the relationship between worship and belief, and is an ancient Christian principle which provided a measure for developing the ancient Christian creeds, the canon of scripture and other doctrinal matters based on the prayer texts of the church, that is, the church's liturgy. In the early church there was liturgical tradition before there was a common creed and before there was an officially sanctioned biblical canon. These liturgical traditions provided the theological framework for establishing the creeds and canon.
>
> The principle is considered very important in Catholic theology. The *Catechism of the Catholic Church* states: "The church's faith precedes the faith of the believer who is invited to adhere

1. Balthasar, *Mysterium Paschale*, 176–79.

to it. When the church celebrates the sacraments, she confesses the faith received from the apostles—whence the ancient saying: *lex orandi, lex credendi.* The law of prayer is the law of faith: the church believes as she prays. Liturgy is a constitutive element of the holy and living Tradition."[2]

Alfeyev. Summary

While the fact that the descent was not itself questioned by representatives of church tradition, there existed various interpretation of this event. Many writers maintained that Christ freed all who were held captive in hell, others thought that only the Old Testament righteous were liberated, and another group believed that only those who came to believe in Christ and followed him were saved. Finally, others held that Christ freed only those who had lived in faith and piety during their earthly lives.

The first interpretation is most widely reflected in the liturgical texts of the Orthodox Church: that Christ "emptied" hell and "not a single mortal" remained. The first and second opinions were endowed with equal authority in the Eastern Christian patristic tradition, but with the passing of the centuries the first gradually gave way to the second. In the Western tradition after Augustine, *the second and fourth views were given preference.*

First of all, belief in Christ's descent into Hades and his preaching to the dead is not a *theologoumenon* [opinion], but belongs to the realm of general church doctrine. The teaching that Christ granted to *all* the possibility of salvation and opened for *all* the doors to paradise should also be considered general church teaching.

Did all or only some follow Christ? Answers to this question belong to the realm of *theologoumena*. The doctrine on salvation formulated by the eastern fathers, particularly by St. Maximus the Confessor and St. John Damascene, can serve as a key to answering this question. According to this doctrine, all are called to salvation but not everyone responds. The only hindrance to salvation is one's free will to resist God's call. Such an understanding radically differs from the doctrine of predestination formed in the Western Augustinian tradition.

2. "Lex Orandi, lex credenda," Wikipedia, https://en.wikipedia.org/wiki/Lex_orandi,_lex_credendi (accessed June 13, 2015).

Christ's preaching in hell, mentioned in 1 Peter 3:18–21, has also been interpreted in different ways. Some writers allowed the possibility that those who did not believe in Christ during their lifetimes could have come to believe in him after their death. Others, mainly Western theologians, rejected this possibility. Some insisted on a literal interpretation: that Christ preached only to the unrepentant sinners from Noah's time. Others interpreted it in a wider sense: that Christ's preaching in hell reached all who were held there. Augustine, and later Western writers, did not consider the Petrine text to refer to the descent into Hades and did not, therefore, believe it should be understood in an allegorical sense. This view does not correspond to any early or Eastern Christian understandings of the passage.

What is universally endorsed is the teaching that Christ mortified death and destroyed hell. This is, however, understood in different ways. The Eastern liturgical texts and many of the fathers speak of a total destruction of death and hell. Others are more specific, saying that death and hell continue to exist but only inasmuch as people's evil wills encourage its existence. In the Western tradition, the view that Christ's death harmed hell but did not mortify it came into dominance.

A great number of Eastern authors perceived Christ's descent into Hades as an event of universal significance, and some extended its saving action not only to past generations but also to all those who followed. The idea that all the dead received the opportunity to be saved is quite widespread among Eastern Christian writers, and it was only in the West where some authors labeled it heretical.[3]

Some Prayers from the Roman Missal for the Salvation of All

One of the main petitions on Good Friday

"Let us pray also for those who do not acknowledge God that, following what is right in sincerity of heart, they may find the way to God himself. Prayer: 'Almighty ever-living God, who created all people to seek you always by desiring you and, by finding you, come to rest, grant, we pray, that, despite every harmful obstacle *all may recognize* the signs of your fatherly

3. Alfeyev, *Christ the Conqueror of Hell*, 204–9.

love and the witness of the good works done by those who believe in you, the one true God and Father of our human race.'"

Prayers of the Easter Vigil

"O God, whose ancient wonders remain undimmed in splendour even in our day, for what you once bestowed on a single people, freeing them from Pharaoh's persecution by the power of your right hand, now you bring about as the salvation of the nations through the waters of rebirth, grant, we pray, that *the whole world* may become children of Abraham and inherit the dignity of Israel's birthright."

"O God, who by the light of the New Testament have unlocked the meaning of wonders worked in former times, so that the Red Sea prefigures the sacred font and the nation delivered from slavery foreshadows the Christian people, grant, we pray, that *all nations*, obtaining the privilege of Israel by merit of faith, may be reborn by partaking of your spirit."

Vigil of Pentecost

"Almighty ever-living God, who willed the Paschal Mystery to be encompassed as a sign in fifty days, grant that from out of the scattered nations the confusion of many tongues may be gathered by heavenly grace into *one great confession* of your name."

Feast of Christ the King

"Almighty ever-living God, whose will is to restore all things in your beloved Son, the King of the universe, grant, we pray, that *the whole creation*, set free from slavery, may render your majesty service and ceaselessly proclaim your praise."

"As we offer you, O Lord, the sacrifice by which the human race is reconciled to you, we humbly pray that your son himself may bestow *on all nations* the gifts of unity and peace." Eucharistic Prayer III

"Listen graciously to the prayers of this family whom you have summoned before you: in your compassion, O merciful Father, gather to yourself *all your children* scattered throughout the world."

Liturgy of the Hours, Tuesday, Mid-afternoon Prayer

"Father, you sent your angel to Cornelius, to show him the way to salvation. Help us to work generously for the salvation of the world so that your church may bring us and all mankind into your presence."

Offertory Prayer 8

"Father, you are the source of the life that your son Jesus Christ secured for us in his death and his Resurrection. Receive us *and all men* into the sacrifice of redemption and sanctify us in the blood of your son."

Weekday Mass, Tuesday, Offertory Prayer

"Lord our God, accept the offering of your church; and may what each individual offers up to the honor of your name lead to *the salvation of all*."[4]

Rosary Prayer.

It was noted above by Fr. Neuhaus that at the end of every decade of the rosary Catholics say the prayer the angel taught the children at Fatima: "O my Jesus, forgive us our sins, and save us from the fires of hell, and lead *all souls* to heaven, especially those most in need of your mercy."

4. *Roman Missal*, 173, 305, 346–47, 428, 481, 630.

— 10 —

The Freedom of the Person vs. God's Will to Save

One of the major topics in the discussion about *apokatastasis* is the freedom of the human person: if we always remain free, then we are always capable of saying no to God. And there cannot be any kind of dogmatic salvation of everyone because of this possibility. It can therefore only be a *hope and not a surety*.

Before presenting the universalist responses to this problem, I wish to show how dominant the objection of free will to universalism is. I will quote from a major conference on the love of God; and then refer to the one lecture given on this theme of human freedom in reference to universalism.

David Fergusson "Will the Love of God Finally Triumph?"

Fergusson points out the decline in the preaching about heaven and hell, gives some reasons for this, and then states: "If the time is gone when the threat of hell can coral people into church attendance and provide an effective form of social control, then perhaps the church has to learn to express the significance of God's love for human life and conduct, a significance that is reflected in the hope of the world to come."

He considers Barth's position, but concludes (as we have seen others conclude) that Barth's doctrine really leads to universalism, and he does not wish to go that route. He faults Barth's position on the grounds of not giving sufficient scope to human freedom: "The possibility that a human being might freely reject his or her election is hinted at only obliquely by the later Barth. Little scope is given to the possibility that divine sovereignty might be exercised by the gift of a radical freedom that enables the creature absurdly to reject his or her election in Christ." Fergusson then proceeds to give his answer—which is really one of the traditional answers—to the problem of how to present eschatological realities to people today: *we are always free to finally say no to God.*

The section of his lecture we are interested in is entitled "Against Universalism." We must think of our ability to reject God's offer as itself a function of God's love. Universalism is another kind of determinism: "It does not allow any human being the freedom to say 'no' to God. Without some such appeal to deliberate human rejection of God, we can explain the possibility of unbelief only in terms of ignorance or a divine decree. Neither alternative can be consistent with the love of God declared in Scripture."

Fergusson admits that everyone in the long run might freely choose God. "Yet the possibility of freedom being *eternally misused* cannot be discounted, and in any event cautions us against too complacent a view of our own destiny" (my italics).[1]

Thomas Talbott

We have seen that Talbott is one of the most prominent Christian universalists. When he was asked to do the article on universalism in *The Oxford Handbook on Eschatology*, it's significant that he chose to focus primarily on this core issue of human freedom. It remains the most persistent objection to universalism, and I believe this is why he chose to concentrate on it for this important volume.

He briefly states the rejection hypothesis (RH) to universalism: "Some persons will, despite God's best efforts to save them, freely and irrevocably reject God and thus separate themselves from God forever."

> The difficulties with such a view begin to emerge, however, as soon as one examines the choice (or choices) specified in RH more carefully. Suppose that God really is, as Christians have traditionally believed, the ultimate source of every good in life and, in particular, the ultimate source of human happiness, then an

1. Fergusson, "Will the Love of God Finally Triumph?," 194–201.

obvious question arises: why suppose it even possible that someone might freely choose to endure an objective horror and then, after experiencing it, continue to embrace it freely for all eternity? Why suppose this even logically possible when the alternative is eternal bliss?

Even if we should grant the bare logical possibility of RH, moreover, this would not amount to very much. For such a possibility would be quite compatible, first of all, with a *hopeful universalism*: the very real possibility that the infinitely resourceful God will successfully win over all sinners in the end. It would also be compatible with the *epistemic certainty*—based upon revelation, for example—that no one will successfully resist God's salvific will forever.

It would even be compatible with something very much like irresistible grace. For consider this: although it is logically possible, given the normal philosophical view of the matter, that a fair coin would never land heads up, not even once, in a trillion tosses, such an eventuality is so incredibly improbable that no one need fear it actually happening. Nor is RH any less improbable that no one need fear it actually happening, even if it is logically possible.

In working with a sinner S (Shattering S's illusions and correcting S's ignorance), God could presumably bring S to a point, just short of actually determining S's choice, where S would see the choice between horror and bliss with such clarity that the probability of S repenting and submitting to God would be extremely high.

The assumption that sinners retain their libertarian freedom together with the Christian doctrine of the preservation of the saints yields the following result: we can be just as confident that God will eventually win over all sinners (and do so without causally determining their choices) as we can be that a fair coin will land heads up at least once in a trillion tosses.

But the New Testament picture nonetheless warrants, I believe, a stronger view, sometimes called *necessary universalism:* the view that in no possible world containing created persons does God's grace fail to reconcile all of them to himself. I shall argue that RH is logically impossible, not just incredibly impossible.[2]

Balthasar:

> But between the misdeeds of the creature and goodness of God there is no equilibrium, which means that justice with respect to mercy, indeed, must be virtually a mode of this mercy. That such things as man and world exist at all is by no means due to God's

2. Talbott, *Universalism*, 451–52.

justice but solely to his goodness, and it is not until God's bottomless generosity deigns to create something that viewpoints such as "justice, generosity and mercy" arise and become relevant.

Here we come to deep waters, in which every human mind begins to flounder. Can human defiance really resist to the end the representative assumption of its sins by the incarnate God? If one replies to this confidently and flatly: "Yes, man can do that" and thereby fills hell with naysayers, then the theologians will again have to set up strange distinctions within God's will for grace: there is then a "sufficient grace" characterized as something that, from God's viewpoint, would have to be sufficient for converting the sinner yet is rejected by the sinner in such a way that it is actually not sufficient for achieving its purpose; and an "efficacious grace" which is capable of attaining its goal. On the other hand, we will not be allowed to say that this latter simply takes the sinner's will by surprise, since his assent has to be freely given. Into what sort of darkness are we straying here?

We can be so overwhelmed by grace that we freely consent.

Tentatively we can say this: that the Holy Spirit, the Spirit of absolute freedom, allows us to see, within our free spirit, what our *own* true freedom would be, that is, by confronting us with ourselves, with our own highest possibility. Do you really want to exist forevermore in contradiction with yourself?

Grace can advance as far as that. And if one wishes to keep to the distinction noted above, then one would have to say: grace is "efficacious" when it presents my freedom with an image of itself so evident that it cannot do other than freely seize itself, while grace would be merely "sufficient" if this image did not really induce my freedom to affirm itself but left it preferring to persist in its self-contradiction.

To push on any farther into these deep waters is not permitted us. We have to stop at this observation: *it would be in God's power to allow the grace that flows into the world from the self-sacrifice of his Son to grow powerful enough to become his 'efficacious' grace for all sinners. But precisely this is something that we can only hope for.* (my italics)[3]

3. Balthasar, *Dare We Hope?*, 154–55, 208–10.

St. Benedicta of the Cross (Edith Stein)

The more that grace wins ground from the things that had filled the soul before it, the more it repels the effects of the acts directed against it. And to this process of displacement there are, in principle, no limits. If all the impulses opposed to the spirit of light have been expelled from the soul, then any free decision against this has become infinitely improbable. Then faith in the unboundedness of divine love and grace also justifies *hope for the universality of redemption*, although through the possibility of resistance to grace that remains open in principle, the *possibility* of eternal damnation also persists.

Seen in this way, what were described earlier as limits to divine omnipotence are also canceled out again. They exist only as long as we oppose divine and human freedom to each other and fail to consider the sphere that forms the basis of human freedom. Human freedom can be neither broken nor neutralized by divine freedom, but it may well be, so to speak, outwitted. The descent of grace to the human soul is a free act of divine love. And there are no *limits* to how far it may extend.

Which particular means it chooses for effecting itself, why it strives to win one soul and lets another strive to win it, whether and how and when it is also active in places where our eyes perceive no effects—those are all questions that escape rational penetration. For us, there is only knowledge of the possibilities in principle, an understanding of the facts that are accessible to us.[4]

John A. T. Robinson

This, in my opinion, is another way of speaking about efficacious grace (below). It is a personalist explanation of the problem concerning God's infinite will to save and our human freedom to say no.

We all know times when a man or woman really shows his or her love for us, whether it is in some costing manifestation of forgiveness or self-sacrifice, or in some small act of kindness or consideration, we feel constrained to respond to it—we cannot help ourselves, everything within us tell us that we must. Our defenses are down, the power of love captures the very citadel of our will, and we answer with the spontaneous surrender of our whole

4. Ibid., 218–21.

being. Yet, at the same time, we know perfectly well that we can, if we choose, remain unmoved; there is no physical compulsion to commit ourselves.

Everyone may point to instances in which he has been constrained to thankful response by the overmastering power of love. And yet, under this strange compulsion, has any one ever felt his freedom to be infringed or his personality violated? Is it not precisely at these moments that he becomes conscious, perhaps only for a fleeting space of time, of being himself in a way he never knew before, of attaining a fullness and integration of life which is inextricably bound up with the decision drawn from him by the other's love?

Moreover, this is true, however strong be the constraint laid upon him: or, rather, it is truer the stronger it is. Under the constraint of the love of God in Christ this sense of self-fulfillment is at its maximum. The testimony of generations is that here, as nowhere else, service is perfect freedom. In throwing ourselves into an action on behalf of someone we really love in Christ, our whole personality can become united, our intellect and emotions fused in one all subordinating purpose of the will, in that complete self-determination in which we know, as at no other time, that we are truly free.

When faced by an overpowering act of love, we realize how absurd it is to say that the freedom and integrity of our moral personality are safeguarded only if we set our teeth and determine not to allow ourselves to be won to its service. If, then, we do not lose, but rather find, our freedom in yielding to the constraining power of love, is there anything to be gained for the cause of liberty by demanding that when it is under the control of self-will it shall in the end be stronger than when it is under the control of love?

May we not imagine a love so strong that ultimately no one will be able to restrain himself from free and grateful surrender? If the miracle of the forcing of pride's intransigence, which is no forcing but a gentle leading, can be achieved in one case (St. Paul would say, in my case), who are we to say that God cannot repeat it in all.

Christ, in Origen's old words, remains on the cross so long as one sinner remains in hell. That is not speculation: it is a statement grounded in the very necessity of God's nature. In a universe of love there can be no heaven which tolerates a chamber of horrors, no concentration camp set in the midst of a blissful countryside, no hell for any which does not at the same time make it hell for God. He cannot endure that, for that would be the final mockery of his nature –and he will not.[5]

5. Robinson. *In the End, God*, 105–6, 116.

— 11 —

John Kronen and Eric Reitan: *God's Final Victory*

I HAVE SAVED THIS book until last because, in my studies, it is the very best treatment of the major issues of universalism. It can serve as a kind of summary of the present book. I will first give the authors' summary of the book, and then present their critical views on some of the most basic arguments for the doctrine of hell. The book "clearly is theological. Nevertheless, we regard our project as ultimately philosophical because . . . our primary objective is to show that a Christian belief system that includes the doctrine of universalism is more rationally coherent than one that includes the doctrine of an eternal hell. And the task of examining the rational coherence of alternative world views strikes us as being the essence of philosophy." The book is a bit expensive and not easy reading.

> Our aim in this book is to critique any soteriology which holds that some rational creatures will be forever separated from God. Our aim, in other words, is to systematically challenge the doctrine of eternal hell (DH) in any form. At the same time we defend DH's chief rival, the doctrine of universal salvation (DU), which holds that ultimately all rational creatures will enjoy blessedness in communion with God. More precisely, our aim is to show that, granted certain core Christian principles, *no* form of DH is as plausible as *some* form of DU. We call this a "comparative" defense of DU.
>
> Defenders of hell must overcome the prima facie absurdity of the following conjunction: God loves every one of His creatures

with a profound and unwavering benevolence; and He wills upon some of these creatures the very worst kind of evil conceivable, and He wills that they suffer it for all eternity, even though it cannot possibly do them *any* good, since it never culminates in anything but more of the same.

Defenders of [another] version of the doctrine of hell face different challenges. Because they hold that damnation originates in the creature's own rejection of God, they must accept that some creatures freely reject God forever, and that God cannot legitimately overcome this free rejection of Him (despite potentially infinite time in which to work on their intransigence). That someone created in the divine image, and hence naturally ordered towards the good, should eternally reject the perfect good strikes us as prima facie unlikely, especially if God continues unremittingly to seek the creature's repentance. Furthermore, that an omnipotent and omniscient God should *eternally* fail to find a morally legitimate way to transform an unwilling creature's heart strikes us as prima facie dubious.

However, the problem runs deeper, as can be seen when we focus on the fact that a necessary feature of every species of the doctrine of hell is that the damned are eternally confirmed in moral degeneracy. This is troubling in its own right, but becomes even more troubling when combined with [the theory] which entails that, in God's war against sin, God confronts *ultimate* defeat in the souls of the damned. Despite all His infinite resources, despite infinite time in which to work, despite His perfect knowledge of every nuance of the souls of the damned, despite His unrelenting love, His efforts will be for naught. At least in some human souls, sin will prove more powerful than God.

This rather staggering implication seems unavoidable for any of the "liberal" versions of hell, and is one that we imagine most Christian theologians historically would have responded to with cries of blasphemy. This may be the main reason that the Classical Doctrine of Hell has not disappeared despite its drawbacks. If God's salvific aims simply do not include the damned, then we are no longer driven to the conclusion that God's aims are, in some human souls, ultimately defeated. In the various forms of the Classical Doctrine, the eternal alienation of the damned is directly intended by God and so cannot be viewed as God's failure or defeat. In this view, God prevails over sin in different ways: in the saved, through their sanctification; and in the damned, through their punitive expulsion from the goods of heaven.

However, this way of thinking obscures deep problems that, once again, become evident when we recall that being confirmed in wickedness is a necessary consequence (perhaps the only necessary one) of being deprived of the beatific vision. In the Classical Doctrine, the damned are punished for their wickedness at least in part by being eternally confirmed in wickedness.

To see the magnitude of the difficulties, it may help to reflect on what is so bad about sin. At root, sin is a failure to appropriately value what ought to be valued, and so to fail to express, in action and dispositions, due reverence for the inherent worth of things. The most significant element of sin, in classical theology, is the failure to do this with respect to God, who has infinite inherent worth, and thus ought to be valued above all else. Failure to do so is a moral affront akin to the sociopath's failure to properly value his victim, only magnified in severity by God's infinite worth.

According to the classical doctrine of hell, God responds to this infinite affront against his dignity by deliberately acting to ensure that this affront continues for all eternity. While He could stop it from continuing, He chooses instead to make sure that this most intolerable of all evils persists forever in the souls of the damned by deliberately withholding the necessary condition for bringing it to an end.

Therefore, the defender of any form of the classical version of hell must explain why it would be a demand of justice to bring it about that a criminal never stop committing his crime. We, at least, cannot conceive of any coherent conception of justice under which this would make any sense.[1]

Argument from Efficacious Grace

The authors devote a whole chapter to what they call the argument from efficacious grace. This chapter is the most convincing argument of anything I have read to demonstrate the possibility of universal salvation. They outline the chapter as follows:

1. It is always possible for God to extend to the unregenerate efficacious grace; that is, a form of grace sufficient by itself to guarantee their salvation (i.e., sufficient to bring about all that is necessary for salvation, including relevant subjecting acts such as sincere repentance and conversion).

1. Kronen and Reitan, *God's Final Victory*, 1–2, 25–26.

2. Making use of efficacious grace to save the unregenerate is morally permissible for God, at least when the recipient would not otherwise have been saved.
3. It is therefore possible and permissible for God to save all through the exercise of efficacious grace.
4. If God has amorally permissible means of saving all, then God will save all.
5. Therefore, God will save all.

When God grants efficacious grace, He guarantees conversion and regeneration by putting creatures in a state that influences their motives such that they have every reason to respond favourably to the offer of salvation and no reason not to. We will argue that God has available to Him a morally permissible means of bringing it about that all of a creature's motives uniformly favour conversion.

Aquinas and his later followers suggest two ways in which God could do this: first, by presenting the unregenerate with a direct vision of Himself; second, by presenting them with evidence and/or arguments sufficient to demonstrate the value of union with God, while simultaneously liberating them from bondage to contrary affective states.

From all this it follows that God could guarantee uniform salvation-inducing motives in rational creatures simply by presenting an unclouded vision of Himself. God's doing this certainly seems metaphysically possible, and hence within God's power. And if (as Aquinas maintained) free acts are not random but motivated, it follows that any rational creature presented with the vision of God will freely but inevitably respond affirmatively to the promise of loving union.[2]

Soteriological Agnosticism

The authors of *Victory* mention another theory that they have found among universalists. They have labeled it the *doctrine of soteriological agnosticism* (DSA), and they define it this way:

> Many are drawn to DSA because of the apparent humility of adopting an agnostic posture towards what God might do in response to unrepentant sin. In itself this humility seems praiseworthy; but

2. Ibid., 131–36.

our case against hell did not merely support an agnostic position on whether God would eternally reject any of His creatures. More strongly, we argued that a God anything like the God of traditional Christianity *would not do so.*

Our case against hell systematically challenges arguments whose conclusions are that God either cannot, or will not, *guarantee* the salvation of all. We argued, on the contrary, that God *can and morally may* (and so will, given our previous arguments) guarantee the salvation of all. If this is right, then our arguments do more than just undercut reasons for embracing the doctrine of hell by appeal to human freedom. They also undercut comparable reasons for embracing DSA. In short, if neither respect for freedom nor the demands of justice impose an impediment to God's saving all, then—given the strong prima facie basis for thinking that God would save all barring impediments to doing so—the proper conclusion is not agnosticism but the Doctrine of Universalism.[3]

3. Ibid., 181.

—12—

Related Issues: Annihilation, Private Revelations: the Mystics, Near Death Experiences

Annihilationism

"There remains the third possibility of either the divine annihilation or the dwindling out of existence of the finally lost. This is a very dubious doctrine of Christian theism to sponsor, and not one in which we should acquiesce except for want of any viable alternative."[1]

This comment by Hick provides an opportunity to introduce a solution that is part of the ongoing discussion concerning universalism: annihilationism.

At the end of their study, the authors of *Victory* have a section entitled "Pragmatic concerns." One of them concerns annihilationism.

> This doctrine holds that "rather than preserving the unregenerate in hell, God extinguishes their existence altogether. Rather than allow them to eternally suffer the effects of alienation [from God], God puts them out of their misery, thereby annihilating them as an act of mercy. Our arguments succeed in showing that God need not annihilate them in order to spare them the grim consequences of freely chosen alienation from Him.
>
> "Perhaps, however, the argument is that annihilation is actually more serious than eternal damnation, because non-being is

1. Hick, *Evil and the God of Love*, 378.

> objectively worse than existence in a state of even the most total torment. Does it follow that God would choose the option which expresses His justice . . . (annihilation) [but not His love (by becoming incarnate and dying for their sakes] . . . ? Hardly."[2]

Conditional Immortality

The theory of annihilationism is also called conditional immortality.

John W. Wenham.

> Belief in conditional immortality is the belief that God created Man only potentially immortal. Immortality is a state gained by grace through faith when the believer receives eternal life and becomes a partaker of the divine nature, immortality being inherent in God alone. It is a doctrine totally different from universalism, which I have long believed quite irreconcilable with Scripture. It shares the doctrine of judgment held by the upholders of everlasting torment in almost every particular—except for one tremendous thing: it sees no continuing place in God's world for human beings living on in unending pain, not reconciled to God. The wrath of God will put an end to sin and evil.[3]

Wenham rejects altogether the use of philosophy (which we have seen is the predominant approach of the authors of *Victory*), in attempting to answer the questions of the situation of life after death. He relies totally on Scripture whose obvious meaning is conditionalism.[4]

> I have thought about these things for more than fifty years and for more than fifty years have believed the Bible to teach the ultimate destruction of the lost. I believe that endless torment is a hideous and unscriptural doctrine which has been a terrible burden on the mind of the church for many centuries and a terrible blot on her presentation of the gospel.[5]

2. Kronen and Reitan, *God's Final Victory*, 179–80.
3. Wenham. "The Case for Conditional Immortality," 162.
4. Ibid.
5. Ibid., 190.

Instead of universalism, he chooses annihilationism to avoid this "terrible blot."

Kendall S. Harmon

It is not necessary to go into the varieties of conditionalism (C) and annihilationism (A) that Harmon gives. The specific doctrine he is critiquing—"penal suffering culminating in total extinction"—comes from a book by Edward Fudge, *The Fire That Consumes,* which is considered "the ablest critique of the traditional understanding of hell." Harmon counsels "reverent scepticism about C," and suggests some who hold that position show "an inadequate appreciation for the role of tradition." Harmon basically offers substantial disagreement with how Fudge interprets all the biblical references to the state of the "lost" in terms of annihilation.

> Fudge's examination of the scriptural witness, when combined with his insistence that immortality is not a gift of creation but rather a gift of the resurrection of Christ, seems compelling, but it contains serious weaknesses. First, Fudge's book is methodologically flawed since, when interpreting the New Testament passages, he over emphasizes the Old Testament background at the expense of the intertestamental literature.
>
> A second weakness of Fudge's work is exegetical: he often introduces a chronological lapse of time in New Testament passages which is not there in the texts themselves. It is crucial to see how this move fits in with Fudge's exact position, which he defines as "penal suffering culminating in total extinction."
>
> The third shortcoming of Fudge's book follows closely on the heels of the second: he fails to understand that the apocalyptic images used to the final doom of the ungodly have a single referent, and instead claims that different images refer to differing aspects of the wicked's final fate.[6]

In summary, Harmon would simply deny that there is a strong biblical basis to the doctrine of *apokatastasis.*

6. Harmon, "The Case against Conditionalism," 196–200, 206–10.

Private Revelations

Instead of "private revelation" some theologians are using the term "post-apostolic revelation," which I prefer. When authenticated by the church, a revelation is part of the ongoing gift of prophecy in the church. Rahner says if something is an authentic revelation, how could it be private, that is, how could it be so insignificant that it should be kept private? However, the common teaching is that such revelations are optional and not part of the faith demanded by the church. Even when a revelation is pronounced authentic (i.e., Fatima, Lourdes, the Sacred Heart to St. Margaret Mary), no one is obliged to believe in it.

The Writings of the Mystics

It is important to distinguish between approved revelations and the writings of the mystics. The latter are not revelations but profound insights into our faith. A variety of opinions can be found in these writings in regards to our topic of universalism. St. Augustine is generally considered a mystic, but his views about universalism were quite different from those of Juliana of Norwich! They are personal opinions of the writers. One might describe them as *mystical theologumena*—my own neologism! Just as with the opinions of theologians, these mystical writings are part of the church's ongoing understanding of, and reflection on, the mysteries of the faith. They are not dogma but opinions.

Balthasar on the Variety of *Mystical Testimonies* about Universalism

After speaking about Dante's *Inferno*, he writes:

> Should we not, rather, follow the church Doctor Catherine of Siena when she admitted to her father confessor, the blessed Raymond of Capua, "If I were wholly inflamed with the fire of divine love, would I not then, with a burning heart, beseech my Creator, the truly merciful One, to show mercy to all my brethren?" She spoke, Raymond tells us, in a soft voice to her Bridegroom and said to him: "How could I ever reconcile myself, Lord, to the prospect that a single one of those whom, like me, you have created in your image and likeness should become lost and slip from your hands? No, in absolutely no

case do I want to see a single one of my brethren meet with ruin, not a single one of those who, through their like birth, are one with me by nature and by grace. I want them all to be wrested from the grasp of the ancient enemy, so that they all become yours to the honor and greater glorification of your name."

The Lord replied to her, as she secretly confided to Raymond: "Love cannot be contained in hell; it would totally annihilate hell; one could more easily do away with hell than allow love to reside in it." "If only your truth and your justice were to reveal themselves," the saint replied to this, "then I would desire that there be no longer a hell, or at least that no soul would go there. If I could remain united with you in love while, at the same time, placing myself before the entrance to hell and blocking it off in such a way that no one could enter again, then that would be the greatest of joys for me, for all those whom I love would then be saved."

But precisely at this point, someone will come up with the numerous texts providing evidence that Catherine herself and many other mystics who, in their imitation of Christ, had experiences of eternal-seeming damnation and godforsakenness. And it is precisely here that we are faced with an absolute paradox of Christian love. The hell that is brought before their eyes does not at all produce resignation in them but fires their resolve to resist it more strongly than ever.

To be sure, a real discernment of spirits is necessary here. There are cases in which the saint sees a group of men *heading for hell* (like "snowflakes", or like "falling leave") and throws himself into the breach at the sight of their "course toward hell". There are other cases in which a personal experience of hell is granted apart from the sight of any damned persons; here (as with John of the Cross and Teresa of Avila), it is divine grace that arouses the zeal for representative sacrifice. "From there come, too, the powerful urges to help souls, with the result that it seems to me in truth that I would suffer death a thousand times with the greatest joy in order that even only one single soul might escape so horrible a torment" (Teresa).

Of Little Therese [of Lisieux] Besler rightly says, "It is beyond doubt that the Church's teaching about the *possibility* of eternal damnation was of great concern to her." Even if there were cases not only in which *images* of hell were represented (which in my view, probably applies regarding the vision of hell by the children of Fatima) but also which certain chosen ones had subjective certainty that a number of men were already lost, then still (and this is the intention behind the revelation) the wish to take a stand

> against what was shown, to render it, as it were, untrue, by far outweighs in them the thought that with respect to those shown as lost nothing more can be done.[7]

Julian of Norwich

I am going to offer (below) at least one example of a near-death experience. In these experiences people are drawn *freely* to give themselves to the overwhelming Love they experience. I'm going to suggest that this is the answer to the problem of how can one believe in absolute universalism if people are always *free* to accept or refuse? The answer: *They freely give in to the overwhelming presence and attraction of Love when they experience the Presence of Love.* I mention this here because it is little known fact that Julian's *Showings* were received *in just such an experience.*

Sweetman

> In Julian's case, we know that all but one of her revelations were given to her in the context of a near-death experience, when, *in extremis*, she was presented a crucifix to focus her devotion in the interstice between Viaticum and death.
>
> In commenting on her second showing, Julian identifies three things that God wishes us to have. The third of these things is that we trust God with all our might. "He works in secret, yet he wills to be seen. His appearing will be delightful and unexpected. His will is that we trust him, him who is utterly kind and unassuming. Blessings on Him!"
>
> Commenting on the fourteenth showing she emphasizes that Christ wills that "we trust that he is lastingly with us. For God wills that we should hold on in trust so that here below we may be as sure of our hope of heavenly bliss as we shall be absolutely certain of it when we are there above."
>
> "This word, 'You will not be overcome,' was said very distinctly and firmly to give us confidence and comfort for whatever troubles may come. He did not say, 'You will never have a rough passage, you will never be over-strained, you will never feel uncomfortable,' but he *did* say, 'You will never be overcome.' God wants us to pay attention to these words, so as to trust him always with strong

7. Balthasar, *Dare We Hope?*, 214–16.

> confidence through thick and thin. For he loves us, and delights in us; so he wills that we should love and delight in him in return, and trust him with all our strength. So all will be well."
>
> Julian never tired of saying "all shall be well."
>
> Was Julian a universalist? It would seem not, *if* the term is used to name an intellectual position validly assumed as a result of careful logical analysis. On the other hand, if one were to speak not of an order of reasons but instead of an "order" of hope, one would have to come to a different conclusion. Hope must be universal in its encompass. To Julian's way of thinking, such a position has a great deal of plausibility; it is something one could trust with a trust aimed in love at the God who is Love and who has made us the most marvelous promises.[8]

Catherine of Genoa on Purgatory

Up to this point we have looked at post-apostolic (private) revelations in reference to what they say about people going to hell or possibly everyone being saved. However, we have revelations about other aspects of the afterlife. One of the most remarkable is that of Catherine of Genoa's revelations about purgatory. In the course of my studies I have come to see that her revelations about the purgation people must suffer before they are admitted into the presence of God can very well be understood as that purifying fire that Clement and Origen spoke about. One of their arguments against hell is that God does not punish in a punitive way: God's purification is only for remedial purposes and therefore temporary. This is what the Catholic Church has always understood in her doctrine of Purgatory.

In St. Catherine's revelations about purgatory she gives a very profound description of the purification people must suffer in order to enter the Lord's presence. Realizing their impurity, they willingly accept, and even throw themselves into, the cleansing "fire" in order to see God. With all the caveats concerning private revelations given by Balthasar, I believe Catherine's revelations can be understood as the remedial purification that Clement and Origen and many modern theologians accept as part of our journey to the Father.

An added problem Protestant theologians have about defending universalism is that, at the Reformation, they kept hell but did away

8. Sweetman, "Sin Has Its Place," 69–91.

with purgatory! Catholic theology can give a traditional answer to the remedial purgation postulated by the early Fathers. It is the teaching on purgatory. First, I will give a few doctrinal quotes about purgatory from the church's teaching. (Most people are familiar enough with a general understanding about Purgatory.) Then I will give some beautiful insights from St. Catherine.

Catechism of the Catholic Church

"No. 1030. All who die in God's grace and friendship, but still imperfectly purified, are indeed assured of their eternal salvation; but after death they undergo purification, so as to achieve the holiness necessary to enter the joy of heaven.

"No. 1031. The Church formulated her doctrine of faith on Purgatory especially at the Councils of Florence and Trent. The tradition of the Church, by reference to certain texts of Scripture (1 Cor 3:15; 1 Pet 1:7), speaks of a cleansing fire":

> As for certain lesser faults, we must believe that, before the Final Judgment, there is a purifying fire. He who is truth says that whoever utters blasphemy against the Holy Spirit will be pardoned neither in this age nor in the age to come. From this sentence we understand that certain offenses can be forgiven in this age, but certain others in the age to come. (St. Gregory the Great)[9]

Baron Friedrich von Hugel

For a brief look at Catherine's teaching about Purgatory I turn to the magisterial two-volume study of von Hugel. It is considered the definitive work on Catherine of Genoa. A book-length application of von Hugel's study to the theology of universalism would be a very significant contribution to the discussion. Here I simply wish to make the point that her mysticism of purification can be applied to what Clement and Origen called remedial punishment.

From Catherine's writings as quoted by von Hugel:

> The soul thus seeing (its own imperfection) and that it cannot, because of the impediment (of this imperfection) attain to its own

9. *The Catechism of the Catholic Church*, 268–69.

end, which is God; and that the impediment cannot be removed from it except by means of Purgatory, swiftly and of its own accord casts itself into it.

If the soul could find another Purgatory above the actual one, it would, so as more rapidly to remove from itself so important an impediment, instantly cast itself into it, because of the impetuosity of that love which exists between God and the soul and tends to conform the soul to God.

I see the divine essence to be of such purity, that the soul which should have within it the least mote of imperfection, would rather cast itself into a thousand hells than find itself with that imperfection in the presence of God.

The souls in Purgatory have their (active) will conformed in all things to the will of God; and hence they remain there, content as far as regards their will. As far as their will is concerned, these souls cannot find pain to be pain, so completely are they satisfied with the ordinance of God, so entirely is their (active) will one with it in pure charity.

The souls in Purgatory think much more of the opposition which they discover in themselves to the will of God. I do not believe it would be possible to find any joy comparable to that of a soul in Purgatory, except the joy of the Blessed in Paradise.

The soul approaches more and more to that state of original purity and innocence in which it had been created. The instinct of God, bringing happiness in its train, reveals itself and increases on and on, with such an impetuousness of fire that any obstacle seems intolerable.

The joy of a soul in Purgatory goes on increasing day by day, owing to the inflowing of God into the soul, an inflowing which increases in proportion as it consumes the impediment to its own inflowing.[10]

Jerry Walls on Purgatory

Walls is one of the foremost Protestant (Methodist) theologians writing on eschatology. He edited and wrote the Introduction for the prestigious *Oxford Handbook on Eschatology.* Walls is not a universalist, but it's significant that as a Protestant and as a believer in hell he has come to believe in some kind of remedial and temporary suffering after death. We ordinarily associate the doctrine of purgatory with Catholicism and not with Protestantism.

10. Von Hugel, *The Mystical Element*, 284–90.

However, in an early article significantly entitled "Purgatory for Everyone" Walls reflects on the major theological problem that demands an answer: What about people who die and are still not in a "perfect state" to see God?

Walls takes his cue for his position on purgatory from the Anglican theologian David Brown who argues that real virtue cannot be attained in an instant but must take the gradual pattern as it does in our earthly life. Walls also finds this line of argument in Wesley, the founder of Methodism:

> It is just this sort of consideration that led Wesley to insist that sanctification must normally be preceded by a significant period of growth and maturation. Without this process, one is not prepared to receive the fullness of grace sanctification represents. If his basic line of thought is correct, there is good reason to think that something like the traditional notion of purgatory is indeed necessary for those who have not experienced significant growth and moral progress. Now if God deals with us this way in this life, it is reasonable to think He will continue to do so in the next life until our perfection is achieved.
>
> The doctrine of purgatory makes clear that there is no short-cut to sanctity. While popular images of purgatory may evoke negative thoughts, we should recall that the New Testament frequently teaches Christians to rejoice in the adversity that purifies our faith. This is not to trivialize the pain of purgatory, but rather to point out that it should not be dreaded any more than the pain of moral transformation that we experience in this life.
>
> Indeed, all believers, regardless of tradition, who have experienced as joy the purging involved in drawing closer to Christ can view the concept of purgatory not only as a natural doctrinal development, but also as a gracious gift of love.[11]

This article by Walls was only the beginning of his reflections on purgatory. He finished his trilogy *Hell: The Logic of Damnation*, *Heaven: The Logic of Eternal Joy*, with *Purgatory: The Logic of Total Transformation*. And even more recently he has published *Heaven, Hell, and Purgatory*. Since Walls wrote that early article his later works have only expanded and developed his understanding of purgatory. The following is from his latest book:

> All Christian theological systems have to account for how we become impeccable, how we achieve a settled character such that sin is no longer possible for us. The common Protestant answer is that we get this character at the moment of death when God

11. Walls, "Purgatory," 28–30.

> zaps us and instantly perfects us. The answer given by advocates of the doctrine of purgatory is that God gives us this character as the final stage of sanctification, a process that is carried forward from beginning to end as we exercise faith in cooperation with his grace. I believe there are good reasons for Protestants as well as Roman Catholic to prefer the second answer.[12]

Walls is not a universalist, but in this most recent book he writes:

> [I have written] not only numerous articles but also a full book defending the doctrine of eternal hell. I find myself in the somewhat odd position that I would be delighted if one of the things I have given the most energy defending in my career turned out to be false.
>
> Let me clarify what I mean. The doctrine of eternal hell is an entirely contingent truth in my view. That is to say, I only believe it is true because I believe Scripture teaches that some persons will in fact freely and persistently resist the grace of God and be lost. If I am wrong in following this interpretation of Scripture, it is an open question whether all will be saved. Certainly *in principle all could be saved*, since Christ died for all and God sincerely desires all to be saved."[13]

Adrienne von Speyer

Balthasar received many of his theological inspirations from the mystic Adrienne von Speyer. He said her writings would eventually be more important than his own. In *Theodrama, The Last Act, V*, he has a section called "The Question of Universal Salvation." This was published five years (1983) before *Dare We Hope?* He quotes a number of sayings of von Speyer relevant to universalism. As a mystic, her comments belong in this section of post-apostolic revelation. In the following passage by Balthasar the quotes are from von Speyer. I omit his references to her works for the sake of simplicity.

> As a preliminary we observe that all the Lord's words that refer to the possibility of eternal perdition are pre-Easter words, like John 9:39, where Jesus says that he has come into the world in order to judge it. "This is one of the words of the Lord that are

12. Walls, *Heaven, Hell*, 112–13.

13. Ibid., 109.

spoken before the fact of the redemption on the Cross, at a time when the light has not yet penetrated the whole of the darkness." After Easter the first words we hear are Paul's, full of certainty that, if God be for us, no earthly power can be against us. "The Lord suffers for love of all. Unless God's demands on his Son were divine in character, unless God's acts were unsurpassable, each one surpassing the other, the work of redemption on the Cross could be surpassed by man's negation. But when God makes demands of God he makes sure that God always overtakes man, that grace has more weight than sin, that the redemption is complete."

In John the universality of redemption is stressed with equal emphasis: "Long ago, when the Lord decided to come, he chose us, all of us, in order to redeem us. He took up a work of Redemption that was not designed for individuals only . . . that was meant for all. The Lord died not only for good persons, who open themselves to him at once, but also for the wicked who resist him. He has the time to wait until even these scattered children of God are touched by his light. For not even the wicked person stands outside the sphere of his power, and the dispersion of the Lord embraces and overtakes even the dispersion of the sinners." As the Good Shepherd, he has been commissioned by the Father "to bring back all the sheep, the whole flock, to him," and when he is lifted up, to "draw all men to himself."

And even while he knows of the hatred and indifference of many, "fundamentally he is always talking about everyone. Here he speaks of all mankind as those who do not keep the commandments"; for ultimately "none of them is up to this standard of measurement." So he prays to the Father: "Thou hast given him power over all flesh, to give eternal life to all whom thou hast given him"(Jn 17:2). At first this handing over "to the Son, looks like a restriction . . . but this restriction is straight away abolished": eternal life "belongs originally to the Father," but from all time he has shared it with the Son: "Into this participation the Son leads all those whom the Father has given him, namely all flesh."

"His whole mission will be accomplished only when all will be redeemed from sin and be with the Father." In his Passion he must suffer for all those "who, without him, would have deserved hell." Yet, "the darkness of sin remains enclasped in the darkness of love," as the Son suffers it in being forsaken by God.[14]

There follows a long section entitled "Approaching the Reality of Hell." Balthasar ends this section by quoting the Lord's words to several mystics

14. Balthasar, *The Last Act*, 279–82,300–21.

about trusting him completely. His final line is that of *hope* from the Dies Irae: "Through the sinful woman shriven, Through the dying thief forgiven, Thou to me a hope hast given." He will expand on this theme of hope in *Dare We Hope?*

Near-Death Experiences

Hundreds of thousands of people are having experiences of what Robinson described (above). They enter the Presence of an overwhelming Love that is totally accepting, non-judgmental, inviting, and they *freely give themselves to this Presence.* There is a growing field of study about these experiences. Dr. Ken R. Vincent is one of the foremost leaders in this field.

Vincent

> Of all the theological explanations for the near-death experience (NDE), *the Doctrine of Universal Salvation, also known as Universalism is the most compatible with contemporary NDE accounts.* [my emphasis] Universalism embraces the idea that God is too good to condemn humankind to Eternal Hell and that, sooner or later, all humanity will be saved. Interestingly, a belief in Universal Salvation can be found in virtually all the world`s major religions. In this chapter I want to show that Christian Universalism, a doctrine with solid support in the New Testament, blends seamlessly with the experience of near-death experience.
>
> I hope to offer a source of comfort not only to the general reader, but also specifically to near-death experiences, both Christian and non-Christian, who may have had their experience marginalized by assaults from Fundamentalist or Conservative Christians. They can be assured of a more loving alternative to Christian "exclusivity" (i.e., "only Christians go to Heaven") exists within the same *New Testament* they have known since childhood.[15]

Vincent gives some examples of how near-death experiences correspond to Scripture:

> God is light (1John 1:5). One of the most commonly reported characteristics of a deep NDE is the experience of Light or Being of Light. "I was in the Universe and I was Light. It takes all the fear of dying out of you. I went directly into the Light."

15. Vincent, *Thread,* 53.

God is love (1 John 4:7–8). "I left my body, and I was surrounded by God. It didn't feel male or female, young or old, just me. I was surrounded by Love. It is something which becomes you and you become it. I could say I was peace; I was love."

For in him we live and move and have our being (Acts 17:28). "The light was in me and between the molecules, the cells in my body. He was in me—I was in him. I knew all things. I saw all things. I was all things. But not me; Jesus had this. As long as I was 'in Him' and he was 'in me,' I had this power, this glory."[16]

Rachel Noam

The following experience happened to a young Israeli woman who was walking past a construction site and was hit on the head by a falling piece of lumber. She died medically, and this is part of her experience during her unconsciousness.

> The entire experience filled me with an indescribable sense of exalted happiness. I saw the blinding luminescence, glowing in a soft velvety white, as if an infinite number of brightly flashing magic sparks were uniting in a burst of spectacular brilliance.
>
> The magnificent stream of light was accompanied by a flow of sublime love, a kind of love I had never before experienced. It was unlike the love of parents toward their children, the love of friends and relatives or the love of Eretz Yisrael [her fiancé]. Any love I had ever felt was nothing but a tiny speck compared to this exalted, powerful love. Even if all the sparks of love that abound in this world were to combine they could not equal the powerful, pure love I sensed. There was no possibility of evading the current of love that enwrapped me. No words can describe the enchantment, the wonder, the incomparable, infinite goodness. I discerned in it qualities of a passion, spiritual pleasure, strength, happiness and beauty in infinite profusion.
>
> I felt a powerful bond with this marvelous presence. This was the will of a higher Power, a Being of infinite might. I felt a strong pull to become part of this wonderful eternal flow. It attracted me like a magnet with the power of its goodness, just as the earth exerts its attraction on the physical body. This magnetic force consisted of a confluence of goodness, light, faith, pleasure, self-effacement, joy, love, compassion, beauty, hope and favor that

16. Vincent, *Thread*, 57–58.

> drew me closer with its overwhelming magnetism. Filled with awe and reverence I turned to the wonderful Being and told Him about the extraordinary attraction over me.[17]

It is not necessary for my purpose to go into any other details of such experiences. The main point is that thousands of people are "returning" from their near death experiences and giving similar testimonies of meeting an overwhelming Personal Presence of Love to whom they are attracted to *freely give themselves.* I am suggesting to the reader that these personal testimonies are *experiential arguments* to answer the problem of free will versus God's will.

Experiences of *Efficacious Grace.*

Many opponents of universalism argue that we are always free and so we can always say no to God. But God "outwits us" (Edith Stein) by *freely* overpowering us by the Presence of Divine Love. And we recall that one of the possibilities presented by Aquinas for converting people was by presenting the unregenerate with a direct vision of him.

Eric Stetson

The vast majority of Near-Death Experiences (NDE) are filled with light and peace and love. I am using these experiences as an argument for how the human will can be *freely* overcome by Love. One common objection to this near-death argument is that not all these experiences are so wonderful. Stetson has some important reflections on some frightful experiences of "hell" in NDE. His reflections would also apply to other such experiences or "visions of hell" that people report.

> Visions and mystical experiences of heaven and hell are a dime a dozen. For every vision of a stereotypical hell of eternal torture, there are visions of a heaven where all people are saved. Basing our theology and beliefs about the afterlife primarily on visionary experiences that people claim to have had is not a good idea.
>
> The phenomenon of near-death experiences in which a person's spirit seemingly leaves the body and hovers over it, then journeys to other dimensions while the body and brain are clinically

17. Rachel Noam, "The View from Above," http://www.chabad.org/library/article_cdo/aid/3157/jewish/The-View-from-Above.htm (accessed June 13, 2015).

dead, is well documented. Only a small minority of NDE reports are of the hellish variety. In most cases, people say they went to a place of light and peace rather than darkness and suffering.

The few cases where people go to hell and return to tell the tale actually support the idea that God lets people out of hell rather than keeping them there eternally. Most NDE testimonies that include a trip to hell also include God responding to the lost soul's prayers, upon which the negative experience generally transforms into a positive one. Stories like these show that hell is not eternal, since people who go there are given the opportunity to escape, and do in fact leave when they are ready for repentance and God is ready to release them. Why else would the dead man on the operating table suddenly, miraculously come back to life and return with a story of going to hell, if not because God was merciful and allowed him another chance?

There are two things that the vast majority of near-death experiences seem to teach people about God and the afterlife: first, that there is a God who loves us more than we could even imagine; and second, that judgment and hell are real but not eternal. Most people who have an NDE come back as believers in a benevolent Higher Power and life after death, and embrace the teaching of universal salvation—specifically, a concept of restorative universalism, that the soul must only be purged of evil in order to enter heaven.

Very few NDEs convince people that there is such a thing as eternal damnation. In fact, eternal damnation is probably the number one traditional Christian doctrine that people *reject* after having such an experience!

One feature of many near-death experiences is that the visions people see of the afterlife tend to correlate with their own expectations or beliefs, and are designed to challenge them in some way in their life using imagery that would be strongly motivating to that particular individual. In other words, *NDEs seem to be tailored to each person's spiritual understanding and needs, rather than a uniform presentation of absolute truth.* [my italics]

This suggests that some NDE visions of hell could be primarily designed to frighten people into changing their lifestyle—to stop sinning and become more righteous in their behavior. Perhaps some people can only be moved to change their ways by seeing horrible visions of hell, and that is why God allows the experience. We cannot draw general theological conclusions from them.[18]

18. Stenson, *Christian Universalism*, 73–75.

I remember reading years ago in a brief history of stigmatists that people received the wounds of Christ in the form and bodily position corresponding to the crucifix before which they prayed. In other words, the wounds corresponded to their understanding, and so there were often contradictory "revelations" about the place and nature of the wounds. This suggests that "visions" are given according to the person's understanding at the time of the vision. They are not meant to be true historical or dogmatic revelations. This understanding of revelations would apply as well, therefore, to a person's understanding of heaven, hell, and purgatory. Catherine of Genoa's visions would correspond to her traditional understanding of these aspects of her faith.

Carol Zaleski

It is significant that the editors of the *Oxford Handbook of Eschatology* included a study of near-death experiences. Evidently they also see such experiences as having a bearing on our understanding of the last things.

Carol Zaleski makes the same point that these experiences more or less correspond to the person's understanding. She relates medieval NDE experiences that conform more or less to Dante's traditional imagery. Then she says:

> Today, however, popular near-death accounts are more concerned with overcoming fear of death than with warning the reader about postmortem punishment. The life review has lost its sting; a renovated postmortem tribunal, presided over by a most reassuring being of light, conforms to current best practices in education, management, and therapy, and it conveys a message of unconditional acceptance. *Cultural expectations are at work* no less in generic spirituality-and-water versions of near-death experiences than in medieval revenant tales. [my emphasis][19]

A current, pertinent example of how cultural and religious expectations are at work in near-death experiences is given by Zaleski from the life of John Richard Neuhaus. The quotes are from Neuhaus's book *As I Lay Dying*. He speaks in the third person:

> "All of a sudden, I was sitting up in bed staring intently into the darkness." In front of him was a "color like blue and purple vaguely

19. Zaleski, "Near Death Experiences," 621.

> in the form of hanging draperies," and by that drapery he saw two "presences." Without words, they conveyed the message that "everything is ready now." He was quite willing to leave in their company, but the presences departed and the vision ceased, leaving behind an indelible impression.
>
> But the experience did not interpret itself. For that purpose, Neuhaus turned to his Christian formation. The presences, he reasoned, must be angels, messengers of God whose role was to serve as guardians and guides: "I understood that they were ready to get me ready to see God. It was obvious enough to me that I was not prepared in my present physical and spiritual condition, for the beatific vision, for seeing God face to face. They were ready to get me ready. This comports with the doctrine of purgatory."
>
> Thus the experience unfolded in his mind. Not only was he viscerally certain of its reality, but he began to see how it conformed to established Christian doctrine, how it harmonized with other sound works of a sound, deeply informed Christian imagination (especially Newman's *Dream of Gerontius*), and thus how it could be integrated into the life of faith.[20]

A similar explanation is given to the experiences of people who have other beliefs, Hindu, for example:

"Many people have asked me (the webmaster) why experiences such as Hindu near-death experiences are so different than western ones. The reason is because everyone has their own cultural and religious background by which they see their experiences."[21] I think it can be presumed that this explanation applies to everyone, whatever his or her belief system.

An Alternative (Bad) Motivation to Choose God

We have seen above that an overwhelming experience of God is one of the arguments universalists use to resolve the problem of freedom: one can be so overwhelmed as to *freely* choose the Good. Besides an experience of an unconditional love, some universalists argue that God could give another kind of experience that could also induce the person to freely choose the Good. What follows could also be an explanation for "bad" experiences:

20. Ibid., 625.

21. Kevin Williams, "Near-Death Experiences of Hindus," http://www.near-death.com/hindu.html (accessed June 13, 2015).

> God can let them have an immediate experiential encounter with the *alternative* to union with God. If one has a choice between A and not-A, and there is uncertainty about which choice is better, there are two ways to erase such uncertainty. If a demonstration of A's choice-worthiness is unavailable, it may still be possible to demonstrate the supreme unworthiness of choosing not-A. That is, God may not be able to bestow the beatific vision prior to salvation, but that does not mean He cannot let them have the alienation they choose, and so experience fully what it means to exist apart from the source of all that is genuinely valuable.
>
> Perhaps a full experiential understanding of the unworthiness of this choice does not become immediately apparent. Perhaps the unregenerate can, for a time, offset their misery by hoping that a range of illusory goods will satisfy them; but if so, God can let those illusory hopes be fulfilled one by one, thereby shattering them. Therefore, by preserving the unregenerate in being and leaving communion with God an open choice, God can insure that eventually the damned will have every last illusion shattered, and so have an immediate experiential understanding of what it means to reject God, an understanding in which no doubt or uncertainty lingers. They will come to know, wholly and completely, that what they have chosen is utterly without worth, utterly empty; and God's hand will remain extended to them for as long as it takes.[22]

In a NDE God can give a person—as is the case most of the time—a wonderful experience of light and love. However, if for some reason known only to him he deems it more appropriate to give the person a *negative experience*, and in that way have her or him freely choose the Good, God can do so. This could be one explanation of the negative experiences of NDE'rs.

> A few people, such as attempted suicides, do report distressful near-death experiences which Moody describes as being stuck and unable to approach the Being of Light. The consensus of researchers is that such negative experiences are extremely rare. Moreover, such people tend to be depressed when they "die," i.e., their own inner state is a "hellish" one. They also tend to be scrupulous and guilt-ridden—they are the ones who try too hard to be "good" and who least fit the description of those one might expect to find in hell.
>
> Dr. Kenneth Ring found that if a person has a distressful near-death experience and then "dies" again, his or her second experience is always a positive one. Dr. Ring attributes this to a change in consciousness, in which those who cannot at first adjust to the

22. Kronen and Reitan, *God's Final Victory*, 170.

highly positive state described by the most near-death subjects are able to do so by their second experience. We think the change may also be a result of the healing flowing from the first experience.[23]

Ladislaus Boros

In his section on "Apokatastasis in Catholic Theology, Daring Search for New Ways," Deak presents some ideas from Ladislaus Boros, a prominent Hungarian Catholic theologian of the last century. It is the traditional understanding that our final decision concerning our eternal destiny happens *at the moment of death.* Boros expands our understanding of the *moment* of death. In the citation from Deak that follows, I believe we can apply these insights of Boros to the period the NDErs are experiencing: they are somewhat in eternity but have not yet passed over into the *state* of eternity, into their final destiny. They are still able to make decisions, for example, to return to their mortal bodies. This is where Boros places our first really free decision about our destiny. Deak quotes Boros:

> This moment has to lie at the meeting point of time and eternity, neither before nor after. Our existence [in this world] in its stage of multiple distractions is not in a position to throw the whole extent of its being into one single act of realization. That is why our realization of the infinite is never more than an expectant waiting for the infinite. This encounter with the infinite thus presupposes as the condition of its possibility the opening up of the concrete existence in a decision implemented through an act of absolute freedom.[24]

And Deak comments:

> [This moment] has the structure of the angel's decision concerning God, as Thomistic theology generally teaches. Thus the distinguishing feature of Boros's hypothesis from traditional eschatology lies in a dynamic understanding of the moment of death. Whereas traditional eschatology considers man's state in the last moment *before* his death as a decisive—but static—picture of his fate henceforth, Boros allows and even postulates an absolutely free decision on man's part in the moment of his death.[25]

23. Quoted in Linn et al., *Good Goats,* 65.

24. Boros, *The Moment of Truth,* 126, quoted by Deak, *Apocatastasis,* 250.

25. Deak, *Apocatastasis,* 250.

It is frequently pointed out that when we talk about death we are talking about our experience of *dying*; but death itself, that is, the passing over into the other world, is not part of our earthly experience. In the NDErs we have been given testimonies of the experience of *the passing over*, and this is where Boros would place our really free decision about our eternal destiny.

We have seen that some thinkers (Ellul) deny that we have the power to decide our eternal destiny. They are largely speaking about the very inadequate condition of our choosing *in this life*. This is why Boros places this decision at a time when we are in a really free state for the first time in our existence. Deak again:

> In summary, the hypothesis of final decision, as proposed by Boros, postulates a last chance for man *before* entering his final destiny. At this man decides in full knowledge and freedom largely (but not completely) on the basis of his entire life. Theoretically, this decision includes also the possibility of choosing eternal damnation, however remote this possibility seems to be. Therefore this theory does not guarantee automatically universal salvation which would encourage spiritual slothfulness, but rather intends to free man from a *quasi*-fatalistic conception prevalent in conventional Christian eschatology. In other words, the theory of the possibility and necessity of final decision in death removes one of the greatest obstacles to a rightly understood universalism. Consequently, the decision which is due to determine man's eternal fate takes place in eternity itself, free from the temporal and spatial bondage of earthly existence.[26]

In his final summary, Deak puts it this way:

> We believe that the chance for this last decision is given to every human being some time not later and perhaps also not much earlier than in the moments immediately preceding or following his physical death. In other words, only when man has the full knowledge and the clarity of his power of decision can he decide for (or against) his Creator. We do not believe that at this moment a negative decision could be possible. It is the "impossible possibility" of eschatological unbelief which, though unverifiable by our daily experience, seems to be a necessity when fully realized in the moment between God and his creatures: in perfect vision, love, compassion, justice, glory, freedom, submission and bliss.[27]

26. Ibid., 252–54.

27. Ibid., 342.

Deak does not conclude that Boros is teaching an *apokatastasis* doctrine, but his teaching is part of a search for "new ways" to speak about eschatological matters.

What if the universalists are wrong?

You may be fearful, if you have had the stamina to plow through this book (!), that advocating universalism is a dangerous teaching and will harm the simple faith of the people of God. I would like to make my own these words of Gregory MacDonald. It is what I myself heartily believe. Believing in universalism will do little spiritual damage compared to the belief that infinite love would allow any of his children to suffer eternal torment. MacDonald's is another book I highly recommend if you are going to purchase only a few on this topic. The author states:

> The theology outlined in this book is one that espouses a dogmatic universalism, but I must confess to not being 100 percent certain that it is correct. Thus I am a hopeful dogmatic universalist, a non-dogmatic dogmatic universalist.
>
> So what if I am wrong? Well, if I am wrong, then I will have inspired some false hope in the hearts of some people; but I do not think that I will have done any serious damage. I have not produced a theology with a diminished view of God, nor one that will lead people not to worship God. I have not sidestepped the certainty of God's work in Christ, so that the cross and resurrection remain at the heart of the gospel.
>
> I have not reduced the importance of faith in Christ, or the missionary calling of the church. I have not undermined the authority of the bible. I have not "gone soft" on God's wrath nor got rid of hell. I have not tinkered with any of the key doctrines of orthodox Christianity.
>
> I have made a provisional case for accepting universalism, but in the end one must make a wager and take a position. Here I stand, and in the end I can do no other. Belief in universalism is most certainly *not* a requirement for Christian orthodoxy, but neither does it amount to an exclusion from orthodoxy *even if it is wrong.*
>
> In conclusion, let me ask you to hold in your mind traditional Christian visions of the future, in which many, perhaps the majority of humanity, are excluded forever. Alongside that hold the universalist vision, in which God achieves his loving purpose of redeeming the whole creation. Which vision has the strongest

view of divine love? Which story has the most powerful narrative of God's victory over sin? Which picture lifts the atoning efficacy of the cross of Christ to the greatest heights? Which perspective best emphasizes the triumph of grace over sin? Which view most inspired worship and love of God bringing him honor and glory? Which has the most satisfactory understanding of divine wrath? Which narrative inspires hope in the human spirit? To my mind the answer to all these questions is clear, and is why I am a Christian universalist.[28]

28. MacDonald. *The Evangelical Universalist*, 176.

Bibliography

Adams, John G. *Fifty Notable Years, Views of the Ministry of Christian Universalism During the Last Half-Century.* With Biographical Sketeches. Boston: Universalist, 1882.

Alfeyev. Archbishop Hilarion. *Christ the Conqueror of Hell: The Descent into Hades from an Orthodox Perspective.* Crestwood, NY: St. Vladimir's Seminary, 2009.

Ambaum, Jan. "An empty hell? The restoration of all things?: Balthasar's concept of hope for salvation." *Communio.* International Catholic Review (Spring, 1991), 35-52.

Ansell, Nicholas. *The Annihilation of Hell. Universal Salvation and the Redemption of Time in the Eschatology of Jurgen Moltmann.* Eugene, OR: Cascade, 2013.

Babinski, Edward T. "G. K. Chesterton's Universalism." A Pax on Both Your Houses, Feb. 27, 2013. http://paxonbothhouses.blogspot.com/2013/02/gk-chestertons-universalism-by-edward-t.html (accessed June 13, 2015).

Balthasar, Hans Urs von. *Dare We Hope That All Men Be Saved?* Translated by David Kipp. San Francisco: Ignatius, 1988.

———. *Mysterium Paschale: The Mystery of Easter.* Translated with an Introduction by Aidan Nichols. Grand Rapids: Eerdmans, 1993.

———. *Theodrama: Theological Dramatic Theory.* Vol. 5, *The Last Act.* Translated by Graham Harrison. San Francisco: Ignatius, 1998.

Barclay, William. *A Spiritual Autobiography.* Grand Rapids: Eerdmans, 1977.

Barron, Robert. "Response to Ralph Martin." www.catholicnewsagency.com.

Bauckham, Richard. *God Will Be All in All: The Eschatology of Jurgen Moltmann.* Minneapolis: Fortress, 2001.

Benedict XVI, Pope. *Spe Salvi.* www.vatican.va/holy father/benedict xvi/encyclicals (accessed June 13, 2015).

Bonda, Jan. *The One Purpose of God: An Answer to the Doctrine of Eternal Punishment.* Grand Rapids: Eerdmans, 1998.

Brumley, Mark. "Did Hans Urs von Balthasar Teach That Everyone Will Certainly Be Saved?" Catholic World Report, November 21, 2013. www. catholicworldreport. com/item/2735 (accessed June 13, 2015)..

Bulgakov, Sergius. *The Bride of the Lamb*. Translated by Boris Jakim. Grand Rapids: Eerdmans, 2002.

Cameron, Nigel M. de. S, ed. *Universalism and the Doctrine of Hell: Papers Presented at the Fourth Edinburgh Conference on Christian Dogmatics, 1991*. Carlisle, UK: Paternoster, 1992.

Catechism of the Catholic Church. Liguori, MO: Liguori, 1994.

Clement, Olivier. *On Being Human: A Spiritual Anthropology*. London: New City, 2000.

———. *The Roots of Christian Mysticism*. Hyde Park, NY: New City, 1995.

Colledge, Edmund, and James Walsh, eds. *Julian of Norwich. A Book of Showings*, Part 1. Toronto: Pontifical Institute of Medieval Studies, 1978.

Colwell, John. "The Contemporaneity of the Divine Decision: Reflections on Barth's Denial of 'Universalism.'" In *Universalism and the Doctrine of Hell: Papers Presented at the Fourth Edinburgh Conference on Christian Dogmatics, 1991*, edited by Nigel M. de S. Cameron, 139–60. Carlisle, UK: Paternoster, 1992.

Daley, Brian E. *The Hope of the Early Church: A Handbook of Patristic Eschatology*. Grand Rapids: Baker Academic, 2010.

Deak, Esteban. "Apocatastasis: The Problem of Universal Salvation in the Twentieth Century theology." PhD diss., University of St. Michael's College, 1977.

Divine Office: The Liturgy of the Hours according to the Roman Rite. New York: Catholic Book, 1975.

Du Toit, D. A. "Descensus and Universalism: Some Historical Patterns of Interpretation." In *Universalism and the Doctrine of Hell: Papers Presented at the Fourth Edinburgh Conference on Christian Dogmatics, 1991*, edited by Nigel M. de S. Cameron, 73 – 91. Carlisle, UK: Paternoster, 1992.

Dulles, Avery Cardinal. "The Population of Hell." *First Things* (August, 2008).

Ellul, Jacques. *What I Believe*. Grand Rapids: Eerdmans, 1989.

Fergusson, David. "Will the Love of God Finally Triumph?" In *Nothing Greater, Nothing Better, Theological Essays on the Love of God: Papers for the Sixth Edinburgh Dogmatics Conference*, edited by Kevin J. Vanhoozer, 186–202. Grand Rapids: Eerdmans, 2001.

Fiddes, Paul S. *The Promised End: Eschatology in Theology and Literature*. Oxford: Blackwell, 2000.

Florensky, Pavel. *The Pillar and the Ground of Truth, An Essay in the Orthodox Theodicy in Twelve Letters*. Translated by Boris Jakim. Princeton, NJ: Princeton University Press, 1997.

Gavrilyuk, Paul. "The Ontological Universalism of Sergius Bulgakov." In *All Shall Be Well: Explorations in Universalism and Christian Theology from Origen to Moltmann*, edited by Gregory MacDonald, 280–304. Eugene, OR: Cascade, 2011.

Greggs, Tom. *Barth, Origen, and Universal Salvation: Restoring Particularity*. New York: Oxford University Press, 2009.

Gustafson, Richard. "Solovieve's Doctrine of Salvation." In *Russian Religious Thought*, edited by Judith Deutsch Kornblatt and Richard Gustafson, 31–48. Madison: University of Wisconsin Press, 1996.

Hanson, J. W. *Universalism: The Prevailing Doctrine of the Christian Church during Its First Five Hundred Years*. Boston: Universalist, 1899. http://www.tentmaker.org/books/Prevailing.html (accessed June 13, 2015).

Harmon, Kendall S. "The Case Against Conditionalism." In *Universalism and the Doctrine of Hell: Papers Presented at the Fourth Edinburgh Conference on Christian Dogmatics, 1991*, edited by Nigel M. de S. Cameron, 193–224. Carlisle, UK: Paternoster, 1992.

Harmon, Richard R. *Every Knee Should Bow: Biblical Rationales for Universal Salvation in Early Christian Thought*. Lanham, MD: University Press of America, 2003.

Hayes, Zachary. *What Are They Saying About the End of the World?* New York: Paulist, 1983.

Hick, John. *Evil and the God of Love*. Macmillan, 1966.

Hugel, Baron Friedrich von. *The Mystical Element of Religion as Studied in Saint Catherine of Genoa and Her Friends*. 2 Vols. London: Clarke, 1961.

Hvidt, Niels Christian. *Christian Prophecy: The Post-Biblical Tradition*. Oxford: Oxford University Press, 2007.

Jersak, Bradley. *Her Gates Will Never Be Shut*. Eugene, OR: Wipf and Stock, 2009.

John Paul II, Pope. "Does Eternal Life Exist?" In *Crossing the Threshold of Hope*. New York: Knopf, 1994.

Johnson, Thomas. "A Wideness in God's Mercy: Universalism in the Bible." In *Universal Salvation? The Current Debate*, edited by Robin A. Parry and Christopher H. Partridge, 77–102. Grand Rapids: Eerdmans, 2003.

Kornblatt, Judith Deutsch, and Richard Gustafson, eds. *Russian Religious Thought*. Madison: University of Wisconsin Press, 1996.

Kronen, John and Eric Reitan. *God's Final Victory: A Comparative Philosophical Case for Universalism*. New York: Continuum, 2011.

Kuczynski, Janus. "The Universalism of John Paul II and the United Nations: Towards a New Intellectual-Ethical Environment." In *National, Cultural, and Ethnic Identities: Harmony beyond Conflict*, edited by Jaroslav Hroch, David Hollan, and George F. McLean, n. p. Czech Philosohpical Studies 4. http://www.crvp.org/book/Series04/IVA-9/chapter_xii.htm (accessed June 13, 2015).

Kvanvig, Jonathan L. "Hell." In *The Oxford Handbook of Eschatology*, edited by Jerry Walls, 417–25. Oxford: Oxford University Press, 2008.

Linn, Dennis, et al. *Good Goats: Healing Our Image of God*. Mahwah, NJ: Paulist, 1993.

Lombardi, Josephine. *What Are They Saying About the Universal Salvific Will of God?* New York: Paulist, 2008.

Ludlow, Morwenna. *Universal Salvation: Eschatology in the Thought of Gregory of Nyssa and Karl Rahner*. Oxford and New York: Oxford University Press, 2000.

———. "Universalism in the History of Christianity." In *Universal Salvation? The Current Debate*, edited by Robin A. Parry and Christopher H. Partridge, 191–215. Grand Rapids: Eerdmans, 2003.

MacDonald, Gregory, ed. *"All Shall Be Well": Explorations in Universalism and Christian Theology, from Origen to Moltmann*. Eugene, OR: Cascade, 2011.

———. *The Evangelical Universalist*. Eugene, OR: Cascade, 2006.

Marshall, Howard. "The New Testament Does *Not* Teach Universal Salvation." In *Universal Salvation? The Current Debate*, edited by Robin A. Parry and Christopher H. Partridge, 55–76. Grand Rapids: Eerdmans, 2003.

Martin, Ralph. *Will Many Be Saved? What Vatican II Actually Teaches and Its Implications for the New Evangelization*. Grand Rapids: Eerdmans, 2012.

Moltmann, Jurgen. "The Logic of Hell." In *God Will Be All in All: The Eschatology of Jürgen Moltmann*, edited by Richard Bauckham, 43–47. Minneapolis: Fortress, 2001.

Neuhaus, Richard John. "Will All Be Saved?" August 2001, *First Things* (accessed June 13, 2015).

Rachel Noam, "The View from Above." http://www.chabad.org/library/article_cdo/aid/3157/jewish/The-View-from-Above.htm (accessed June 13, 2015).

Oakes, Edward. "Von Balthasar. Hell and Heresy. An Exchange by Alyssa Lyra Pitstick and Edward Oakes, SJ." *First Things* 168 (2006) 29.

O'Collins, Gerald. *Salvation for All: God's other People.* Oxford: Oxford University Press, 2008.

Origen. *On First Principles.* Edited by G. W. Butterworth. Eugene, OR: Wipf and Stock, 2012.

Oxford Handbook of Eschatology. Edited by Jerry L. Walls. New York: Oxford University Press, 2008.

Parry, Robin A. "Postscript: Universalism as a Theologumenon." Theological Scribbles, June 11, 2010. http://theologicalscribbles.blogspot.com/2010/06/postscript-universalism-as-theologumena.html (accessed June 13, 2015).

Parry, Robin A., and Christopher H. Partridge, eds. *Universal Salvation? The Current Debate.* Grand Rapids: Eerdmans, 2003.

Phan, Peter. *Eternity in Time: A Study of Karl Rahner's Eschatology.* London: Associated University, 1988.

———. *Responses to 101 Questions on Death and Eternal Life.* New York: Paulist, 1997.

———. "Roman Catholic Theology." In *The Oxford Handbook of Eschatology*, edited by Jerry L. Wallis, 215–32. New York: Oxford University Press, 2010.

Phan, Peter. *Living into Death, Dying into Life: A Christian Theology of Death and Life Eternal.* Hobe Sound, FL: Lectio, 2014.

Phillips, Michael. "George MacDonald and the Larger Hope, Part 1." Father of Inklings. http://fatheroftheinklings.com/behind-the-wardrobe/topics-on-gods-justice-the-atonement-and-the-potentiality-of-universal-reconciliation/george-macdonald-and-universal-reconciliation-part-1/ (accessed June 13, 2015).

Powys, David J. "The Nineteenth and Twentieth Centuries Debates about Hell and Universalism." In *Universalism and the Doctrine of Hell: Papers Presented at the Fourth Edinburgh Conference on Christian Dogmatics, 1991*, edited by Nigel M. de S. Cameron, 93–138. Carlisle, UK: Paternoster, 1992.

Rahner, Karl. "The Hermeneutics of Eschatological Assertions." Translated by Kevin Smyth. In *Theological Investigations IV*, 323–46. New York: Crossroad, 1982.

———. *Encyclopedia of Theology: The Concise Sacramentum Mundi.* New York: Crossroad, 1975.

Ramelli, Ilaria. *The Christian Doctrine of Apokatastasis: A Critical Assessment from the New Testament to Eriugena.* Leiden: Brill, 2013.

Reitan, Eric. "Human Freedom and the Impossibility of Eternal Damnation." In *Universal Salvation? The Current Debate,* edited by Robin A. Parry and Christopher H. Partridge, 125–42. Grand Rapids: Eerdmans, 2003.

Robinson, John A. T. *In the End, God: A Study of the Christian Doctrine of the Last Things.* Eugene, OR: Cascade, 2011.

Roman Missal. Toronto: St. Joseph, 2011.

Sachs, John R. "Apocatastasis in Patristic Theology." *Theological Studies* 54 (1993) 617–40. http://cdn.theologicalstudies.net/54/54.4/54.4.1.pdf (accessed June 8, 2015).

Sakharov, Nicholas V. *I Love Therefore I Am: The Theological Legacy of Archimandrite Sophrony.* Crestwood, NY: St. Vladimir's Seminary Press, 2002.

Sanders, John. "A Freewill Theist's Response to Talbott's Universalism." In *Universal Salvation? The Current Debate,* edited by Robin A. Parry and Christopher H. Partridge, 169–87. Grand Rapids: Eerdmans, 2003.

Shaw, J. M. *Life after Death: The Christian View of the Future Life.* Toronto: Ryerson, 1945.

Slesinski, Roberti. *Pavel Florensky: A Metaphysic of Love*. Crestwood, NY: St. Vladimir's Seminary Press, 1984.

Stetson, Eric. *Christian Universalism: God's Good News for All People*. Sparkling Bay Books, 2008.

Strange, Daniel. "A Calvinist Response to Talbott's Universalism." In *Universal Salvation? The Current Debate*, edited by Robin A. Parry and Christopher H. Partridge, 145–68. Grand Rapids: Eerdmans, 2003.

Sweetman, Robert. " Sin Has Its Place, But All Shall Be Well: The Universalism of Hope in Julian of Norwich." In *All Shall Be Well: Explorations in Universalism and Christian Theology, from Origen to Moltmann*, edited by Gregory MacDonald, 66–92. Eugene, OR: Cascade, 2011.

Talbott, Thomas. "Christ Victorious." In *Universal Salvation? The Current Debate*, edited by Robin A. Parry and Christopher H. Partridge, 15–31. Grand Rapids: Eerdmans, 2003.

———. "The Just Mercy of God," Universal Salvation. in George MacDonald." In *All Shall Be Well: Explorations in Universalism and Christian Theology, from Origen to Moltmann*, edited by Gregory MacDonald, 219–46. Eugene, OR: Cascade, 2011.

———. "A Pauline Interpretation of Divine Judgement." In *Universal Salvation? The Current Debate*, edited by Robin A. Parry and Christopher H. Partridge, 32–52. Grand Rapids: Eerdmans, 2003.

———. "Towards a Better Understanding of Universalism." In *Universal Salvation? The Current Debate*, edited by Robin A. Parry and Christopher H. Partridge, 3–14. Grand Rapids: Eerdmans, 2003.

———. "Universalism." In *The Oxford Handbook of Eschatology*, edited by Jerry L. Walls, 446–61. New York: Oxford University Press, 2008.

Valliere, Paul. *Modern Russian Theology: Bukharev, Soloviev, Bulgakov: Orthodox Theology in a New Key*. Edinburgh: T. & T. Clark, 2000.

Vanhoozer, Kevin J., ed. *Nothing Greater, Nothing Better: Theological Essays on the Love of God*. Papers for the Sixth Edinburgh Dogmatics Conference. Grand Rapids, 2001.

Vincent, Ken, R. *God Is with Us: What Near-Death and other Spiritually Transformative Experiences Teach Us about God and Afterlife*. http://www.near-death.com/ebooks/nde/God-Is-With-Us.pdf (accessed June 13, 2015).

———. *The Golden Thread: God's Promise of Universal Salvation*. Lincoln, NE: Universe, 2005.

———. *Visions of God from the Near Death Experience*. New York: Larson, 1994.

Walls, Jerry. "A Philosophical Critique of Talbott's Universalism." In *Universal Salvation? The Current Debate*, edited by Robin A. Parry and Christopher H. Partridge, 105–24. Grand Rapids: Eerdmans, 2003.

Ware, Kallistos. *The Inner Kingdom*. Vol. 1 of *The Collected Works*. Crestwood, NY: St. Vladimir's Seminary Press, 2000.

Wenham, John W. "The Case for Conditional Immortality." In *Universalism and the Doctrine of Hell: Papers Presented at the Fourth Edinburgh Conference on Christian Dogmatics, 1991*, edited by Nigel M. de S. Cameron, 161–91. Carlisle, UK: Paternoster, 1992.

Vanhoozer, Kevin J, ed. *Nothing Greater, Nothing Better: Theological Essays on the Love of God*. From the Sixth Edinburgh Dogmatic Conference. Grand Rapids: Eerdmanns, 2001.

Zaleski, Carol. "Near-Death Experiences." In *The Oxford Handbook of Eschatology*, edited by Jerry L. Walls, 614–28. New York: Oxford University Press, 2008.

Made in United States
Troutdale, OR
10/31/2024

24341664R10110